taste of home
Christmas
COOKIES & CANDY

Spice Cutout Cookies, p. 18

Pineapple Coconut Snowballs, p. 95

Nutty Caramels, p. 101

Almond Raspberry Stars, p. 13

Buttery Spritz Cookies, p. 10

Spice Cutout Cookies, p. 18

Spice Cutout Cookies, p. 18

Chocolate Peppermint Bark, p. 61

Chocolate Thumbprint Cookies, p. 20

Chocolate Coated Pretzels, p. 54

Snowflake Cookies, p. 13

Candy Cake Cookies, p. 15

Chocolate Peppermint Bark, p. 61

Chocolate Thumbprint Cookies, p. 20

Spice Cutout Cookies, p. 18

Holiday Truffles, p. 53

Spice Cutout Cookies, p. 18

Chocolate Thumbprint Cookies, p

Buttery Spritz Cookies, p. 10

Cherry Cheese Windmills, p. 16

Snowflake Cookies, p. 13

Mint-Mallow Chocolate Cups, p. 53

Nutty Caramels, p. 101

Spice Cutout Cookies, p. 18

taste of home
Christmas
COOKIES & CANDY

Editors: Amy Glander, Sara Lancaster **Art Director:** Rudy Krochalk **Layout Designers:** Kathy Crawford, Nancy Novak
Content Production Supervisor: Julie Wagner **Proofreader:** Linne Bruskewitz **Editorial Assistant:** Barb Czysz
Indexer: Jean Duerst **Food Director:** Diane Werner RD **Test Kitchen Manager:** Karen Scales
Recipe Editors: Mary King, Christine Rukavena **Recipe Asset Management System:** Coleen Martin (Manager),
Sue A. Jurack (Specialist) **Test Kitchen Assistant:** Rita Krajcir
Studio Photographers: Rob Hagen (Senior), Dan Roberts, Jim Wieland, Lori Foy
Food Stylists: Sarah Thompson (Senior), Kaitlyn Basasie, Alynna Malson (Assistant), Shannon Roum (Assistant)
Set Stylists: Jennifer Bradley Vent (Senior), Stephanie Marchese (Senior), Dee Dee Jacq, Melissa Haberman, Leah Rekau (Assistant)
Photo Studio Coordinator: Kathleen Swaney

Senior Editor/Books: Mark Hagen **Creative Director:** Ardyth Cope **Vice President, Executive Editor/Books:** Heidi Reuter Lloyd
Senior Vice President, Editor in Chief: Catherine Cassidy **President, Food & Entertaining:** Suzanne M. Grimes
President and Chief Executive Officer: Mary G. Berner

Cover Photography: Gretchen Trautman (Art Director), Jim Wieland (Photographer), Jennifer Janz (Food Stylist)
Cover Background Graphic: Psycho/Shutterstock.com

International Standard Book Number (10): 0-89821-604-4
International Standard Book Number (13): 978-0-89821-604-2
Library of Congress Control Number: 2008928979

taste of home
Christmas
COOKIES & CANDY

Celebrate
the Season with *217*
Yuletide Sensations

Merry Christmas! It's time to gather with family and friends, share some good cheer and welcome the holidays with laughter, fun and plenty of scrumptious delights.

When it comes to festive get-togethers, nothing warms hearts faster than a platter of home-baked goodies and sweet surprises. Whether they feature seasonal specialties or classic confections, bountiful cookie trays always make the holidays jolly and bright.

From clever cutouts and whimsical bites to chocolate candies and fruit-topped nibbles, tooth-tingling favorites are a hallmark of the holiday season…and you'll find all of them within the pages of *Taste of Home Christmas Cookies & Candy*.

Whip up these merry morsels to add magic to your holiday traditions…or any event where a tantalizing treasure is needed. Whether you plan to swap these goodies in a cookie exchange, serve them as a tempting treat at friendly potlucks or simply stack them high on a Santa's cookie platter, *Taste of Home Christmas Cookies & Candy* is sure to be a cherished keepsake for years to come.

Table of Contents

Deck *the* Halls!

Christmas Cookies & Candy makes a great gift for those who love holiday baking. To order additional copies, specify item number 38243 and send $15.99 (plus $4.99 shipping/processing for one book, $5.99 for two or more) to: Shop Taste of Home, Suite 176, P.O. Box 26820, Lehigh Valley, PA 18002-6820. To order by credit card, call toll-free 1-800/880-3012.

CUTOUT & SHAPED COOKIES 1

Awaken your inner artiste with these festive cutout and shaped cookie treasures. From quick-and-easy bites to decorative showstoppers, these delicious recipes will add sweet magic to the holidays.

BUTTERSCOTCH EGGNOG STARS

Butterscotch Eggnog Stars

❄ Cheryl Hemmer, Swansea, Illinois

These yellow star-shaped cookies with a "stained-glass" center are almost too gorgeous to eat. Although they take a little time and patience to prepare, they're worth every minute!

      2/3 cup butter, softened
        1 cup sugar
        1 egg
      1/4 cup eggnog
        2 cups all-purpose flour
      3/4 teaspoon baking powder
      1/4 teaspoon salt
      1/4 teaspoon ground nutmeg
      1/2 cup crushed hard butterscotch candies
OPTIONAL ICING:
  1-1/2 cups confectioners' sugar
      1/4 teaspoon rum extract
        2 to 3 tablespoons eggnog
Yellow colored sugar

In a large bowl, cream butter and sugar. Beat in egg and eggnog. Combine the flour, baking powder, salt and nutmeg; gradually add to creamed mixture and mix well. Divide dough in half.

On a lightly floured surface, roll out one portion at a time to 1/4-in. thickness. Cut with a floured 3-1/2-in. star cutter. Cut out centers with a 1-1/2-in. star cutter. Line baking sheets with foil; grease foil.

Place large star cutouts on prepared baking sheets. Sprinkle 1 teaspoon candy in center of each. Repeat with remaining dough; reroll small cutouts if desired. Bake at 375° for 6-8 minutes or until edges are golden. Cool on baking sheets for 5 minutes. Carefully slide foil and cookies from baking sheets onto wire racks to cool.

For icing, if desired, beat confectioners' sugar, rum extract and enough eggnog to achieve drizzling consistency. Drizzle over cooled cookies if desired. Sprinkle with colored sugar if desired. Let stand until hardened.

Yield: about 3 dozen.

Editor's Note: This recipe was tested with commercially prepared eggnog.

Cream Cheese Dainties

❄ Lynne Stewart, Julian, Pennsylvania

The soft cream cheese makes these tender treats melt in your mouth. Select spreadable fruit or preserves of your choice for a fruity punch.

        1 cup butter, softened
        1 package (8 ounces) cream cheese, softened
  2-1/2 cups all-purpose flour
      1/2 cup apricot spreadable fruit or seedless
             raspberry preserves

In a large bowl, cream the butter and cream cheese. Gradually add flour to the creamed mixture. Divide dough into four portions; cover and refrigerate until easy to handle.

On a lightly floured surface, roll one portion of dough at a time into a 10-in. x 7-1/2-in. rectangle. Trim edges if necessary. Cut into 2-1/2-in. squares.

Place 1/4 teaspoon spreadable fruit or preserves near each end of two diagonal corners. Moisten the remaining two corners with water; fold over and press lightly.

Place onto ungreased baking sheets. Bake at 350° for 12-15 minutes or until corners are lightly browned. Cool 2-3 minutes before removing to wire racks to cool.

Yield: 4 dozen.

CREAM CHEESE DAINTIES

LEMON DREAMS

Spoon 1/2 teaspoonful into each cookie. Dust with confectioners' sugar if desired.

Yield: 3 dozen.

Peppermint Twist Kisses

❄️ **Traci Wynne, Falls Church, Virginia**

As rosy as Santa's cheeks, these merry morsels with the chocolate kiss on top are a delightful Yuletide favorite and one of my most-requested recipes.

1/2	cup butter, softened
1/3	cup sugar
1	egg yolk
1/2	teaspoon peppermint extract
1/2	teaspoon vanilla extract
1-1/4	cups all-purpose flour
1/4	teaspoon salt
4	to 8 drops red food coloring
36	chocolate kisses

In a large bowl, cream butter and sugar. Add the egg yolk and extracts; mix well. Combine flour and salt; gradually add to creamed mixture. Divide dough in half; tint one portion red. Divide each into four portions. Cover and refrigerate for 1 hour.

Shape each portion into a 9-in. log. Place one red log next to one white log; twist gently to create one swirled roll. Roll gently until roll becomes one log. Repeat with remaining dough.

Cut each log into nine slices; roll each into a ball. Place 1 in. apart on ungreased baking sheets. Flatten slightly with a glass. Bake at 350° for 10-12 minutes until edges are lightly browned. Press chocolate kisses into the center of warm cookies. Remove to wire racks to cool.

Yield: 3 dozen.

Lemon Dreams

❄️ **Karen Scaglione, Nanuet, New York**

This buttery cookie with a luscious lemon filling is simply too hard to resist. Every time I serve these elegant bites, I'm asked for the recipe.

1	cup butter, softened
1/3	cup confectioners' sugar
1	teaspoon vanilla extract
1-2/3	cups all-purpose flour

FILLING:

2/3	cup sugar
1-1/2	teaspoons cornstarch
1/4	teaspoon salt
3	tablespoons lemon juice
1	egg, beaten
1	tablespoon butter, melted
1	teaspoon grated lemon peel

Confectioners' sugar, optional

In a small bowl, cream butter and confectioners' sugar until light and fluffy. Beat in vanilla. Gradually add flour and mix well. Cover and refrigerate for 30 minutes or until easy to handle.

Roll into 1-in. balls. Place 2 in. apart on ungreased baking sheets. Using the end of a wooden spoon handle, make an indentation in the center of each.

Bake at 350° for 12-14 minutes or until lightly browned. Remove to wire racks to cool.

For filling, in a large saucepan, combine the sugar, cornstarch and salt. Stir in lemon juice until smooth. Cook and stir over medium-high heat until thickened and bubbly. Reduce heat to low; cook and stir for 2 minutes longer. Remove from the heat. Stir a small amount of hot filling into egg; return all to the pan, stirring constantly. Bring to a gentle boil; cook and stir for 2 minutes. Remove from the heat; gently stir in butter and lemon peel. Cool.

PEPPERMINT TWIST KISSES

MOCHA COOKIE PRETZELS

Mocha Cookie Pretzels

❄ Taste of Home Test Kitchen

If you're looking for a little something special to bake up for the holidays, try these fun mocha-frosted cookies. They make an eye-catching addition to any cookie platter.

- 1/2 cup butter, softened
- 1/2 cup sugar
- 1 egg
- 2 squares (1 ounce *each*) unsweetened chocolate, melted and cooled
- 1 teaspoon vanilla extract
- 2 cups cake flour
- 1/4 teaspoon salt

GLAZE:

- 1 cup (6 ounces) semisweet chocolate chips
- 1 teaspoon shortening
- 1 teaspoon light corn syrup
- 1 cup confectioners' sugar
- 3 to 5 tablespoons hot brewed coffee
- 2 squares (1 ounce *each*) white baking chocolate, chopped

Green colored sugar, optional

In a small bowl, cream butter and sugar. Beat in egg. Beat in melted chocolate and vanilla. Combine flour and salt; gradually add to the creamed mixture. Cover and refrigerate for 1 hour or until dough is easy to handle.

Divide dough into fourths; divide each portion into 12 pieces. Shape each piece into a 6 in. rope; twist into a pretzel shape. Place 1 in. apart onto lightly greased baking sheets. Bake at 400° for 7-9 minutes or until set. Remove to wire racks to cool.

For glaze, in a microwave, melt the semisweet chips, shortening and corn syrup; stir until smooth. Stir in confectioners'

sugar and enough coffee to achieve a glaze consistency. Dip cookies in glaze; allow excess to drip off. Place on waxed paper until set.

In a microwave, melt white chocolate; stir until smooth. Drizzle over cookies. Decorate with red or green sprinkles if desired; let stand until set.

Yield: 4 dozen.

Rosettes

❄ Rita Christianson, Glenburn, North Dakota

Shaped like delicate snowflakes, these crisp rosettes are a lovely winter dessert. I make the Norwegian treats for Christmas and other special occasions.

- 2 eggs
- 1 cup milk
- 1 teaspoon sugar
- 1/4 teaspoon salt
- 1 cup all-purpose flour

Oil for deep-fat frying
Confectioners' sugar

In a small bowl, beat eggs, milk, sugar and salt. Add flour; beat until smooth. In a deep-fat fryer or electric skillet, heat 2-1/2 in. of oil to 375°. Place rosette iron in hot oil for 30 seconds.

Blot iron on paper towels, then dip iron in batter to three-fourths the way up the sides (do not let batter run over top of iron). Immediately place in hot oil; loosen rosette with fork and remove iron. Fry for 1-2 minutes on each side or until golden brown. Remove to a wire rack covered with paper towels. Repeat with remaining batter. Sprinkle with confectioners' sugar before serving.

Yield: about 2-1/2 dozen.

ROSETTES

LOLLIPOP COOKIES

Bake at 375° for 7-8 minutes or until lightly browned. Remove to wire racks to cool.

For frosting, combine the sugar, extract, salt and enough milk to achieve spreading consistency. Frost chocolate cookies. Place a wooden stick on each cookie, leaving 3 in. for handle. Top each with a plain cookie. Frost tops; sprinkle with candies.

Yield: 3 dozen.

Jeweled Thumbprints

❄️ Maria Debono, New York, New York

When I moved here from Malta more than 20 years ago, a kind neighbor lady took me under her wing and baked many cookies for me. This is one of her recipes I will always treasure.

> 3/4 cup butter, softened
> 3/4 cup confectioners' sugar
>   1 egg yolk
> 1/2 teaspoon almond extract
> 1-3/4 cups all-purpose flour
> 1/2 cup raspberry *or* apricot preserves

In a bowl, cream butter and sugar. Beat in egg yolk and extract. Gradually add flour. Cover and refrigerate for 2 hours or until easy to handle.

Roll into 3/4-in. balls. Place 1 in. apart on greased baking sheets. Using the end of a wooden spoon handle, make an indentation in the center of each ball.

Bake at 350° for 12-14 minutes or until edges are lightly browned. Remove to wire racks to cool. Fill with preserves.

Yield: 6 dozen.

Lollipop Cookies

❄️ Jean Edwards, Indianapolis, Indiana

You can use your imagination with this recipe to create designs for any season—the possibilities are endless! Cookie "lollipops" are always a hit with kids.

>   1 cup butter, softened
> 1-1/2 cups confectioners' sugar
>   1 egg
>   1 teaspoon vanilla extract
> 1/4 to 1/2 teaspoon almond extract
> 2-1/2 cups all-purpose flour
>   1 teaspoon baking soda
>   1 teaspoon cream of tartar
>   2 squares (1 ounce *each*) semisweet chocolate, melted

FROSTING:
>   1 cup confectioners' sugar
> 1/4 to 1/2 teaspoon almond extract
> 1/4 teaspoon salt
>   1 to 2 teaspoons milk

Red-hot candies and red sprinkles

In a large bowl, cream butter and confectioners' sugar until light and fluffy. Beat in egg and extracts. Combine the flour, baking soda and cream of tartar; gradually add to the creamed mixture and mix well. Divide dough in half; stir chocolate into one half. Refrigerate for 2 hours or until easy to handle.

On a lightly floured surface, roll out each portion to 1/8-in. thickness. Cut with a 2-1/2-in. cookie cutter. Place 1 in. apart on lightly greased baking sheets.

JEWELED THUMBPRINTS

BUTTERY SPRITZ COOKIES

Buttery Spritz Cookies

❄ Beverly Launius, Sandwich, Illinois

These tender little cookies are very eye-catching on my Christmas cookie tray. The dough is easy to work with, so it's fun to make these into a variety of festive shapes.

1	cup butter, softened
1-1/4	cups confectioners' sugar
1	egg
1	teaspoon vanilla extract
1/2	teaspoon almond extract
2-1/2	cups all-purpose flour
1/2	teaspoon salt

Food coloring, optional
Colored sugar and decorating candies, optional

In a large bowl, cream butter and confectioners' sugar until light and fluffy. Beat in egg and extracts. Combine flour and salt; gradually add to creamed mixture. Tint with food coloring if desired.

Using a cookie press fitted with the disk of your choice, press dough 2 in. apart onto ungreased baking sheets. Decorate as desired.

Bake at 375° for 6-8 minutes or until set (do not brown). Remove to wire racks to cool.

Yield: 7-1/2 dozen.

Cinnamon Sugar Cookies

❄ Leah Costigan, Otto, North Carolina

My mom always had these cookies on hand. They're absolutely delicious with a cup of hot chocolate in the winter or milk in the summer.

1	cup butter, softened
1	cup sugar
1	cup confectioners' sugar
1	cup vegetable oil
2	eggs
1	teaspoon vanilla extract
4-1/3	cups all-purpose flour
1	teaspoon salt
1	teaspoon baking soda
1	teaspoon cream of tartar
1	teaspoon ground cinnamon
1	cup finely chopped pecans, optional

Colored sugar, optional

In a large bowl, cream the butter, sugars and oil. Add eggs and vanilla; mix well. Add flour, salt, baking soda, cream of tartar and cinnamon. Stir in the pecans if desired. Cover and refrigerate for 3 hours or until easy to handle.

Roll into 1-in. balls. Place on greased baking sheets; flatten with the bottom of a drinking glass dipped in sugar. Sprinkle with colored sugar if desired.

Bake at 375° for 10-12 minutes or until set.

Yield: about 8 dozen.

Cardamom Swedish Rusks

❄ Julianne Johnson, Grove City, Minnesota

Cardamom, which has a lemony ginger flavor, is a popular spice in Scandinavian foods and gives a pleasantly pungent flavor to this recipe. Similar to biscotti, these cookies are great "dunkers" for a cup of steaming coffee.

1	cup butter, softened
1	cup sugar
2	eggs
1	tablespoon heavy whipping cream
3/4	teaspoon almond extract
3	cups all-purpose flour
1	teaspoon baking powder
1/2	to 3/4 teaspoon ground cardamom
1/2	teaspoon salt
1/8	teaspoon baking soda

In a bowl, cream butter and sugar. Add eggs, cream and extract. Combine the remaining ingredients; gradually add to creamed mixture (batter will be thick).

Spoon into three greased 5-3/4-in. x 3-in. x 2-in. loaf pans. Bake at 350° for 35-40 minutes or until a toothpick inserted near the center comes out clean. Let cool in pans for 10 minutes.

RASPBERRY RIBBONS

until lightly browned. Cool for 2 minutes. Remove to a cutting board; cut into 3/4-in. slices. Place on wire racks.

In a small bowl, combine glaze ingredients. Drizzle over warm cookies. Cool completely.

Yield: about 5 dozen.

Chocolate-Dipped Spritz

❄ Nancy Ross, Alvordton, Ohio

My sisters and I get together for a weekend during the holidays to do nothing but bake cookies. These chocolate-dipped treats always make an appearance in the goody baskets we give as gifts.

      1   cup butter, softened
    3/4   cup sugar
      1   egg
      1   teaspoon vanilla extract
  2-1/4   cups all-purpose flour
    1/2   teaspoon salt
    1/4   teaspoon baking powder
     11   ounces dark, white *or* milk chocolate candy
          coating
Crushed peppermint candies

In a large bowl, cream butter and sugar. Beat in egg and vanilla. Combine the flour, salt and baking powder; gradually add to creamed mixture.

Using a cookie press fitted with the disk of your choice, press dough 2 in. apart onto ungreased baking sheets. Bake at 375° for 7-9 minutes or until set (do not brown). Remove to wire racks to cool.

In a microwave-safe bowl, melt candy coating; dip each cookie halfway. Sprinkle with crushed candies. Place on waxed paper until set.

Yield: about 6 dozen.

Remove to a cutting board; cut each loaf into nine slices with a serrated knife. Place cut side down on an ungreased baking sheet. Bake for 10 minutes. Turn slices; bake 10 minutes longer or until crisp and golden brown. Remove to wire racks to cool. Store in an airtight container.

Yield: 27 cookies.

Raspberry Ribbons

❄ Patsy Wolfenden, Golden, British Columbia

I make these attractive, buttery cookies every holiday to serve at our remote guest lodge. All the girls who help in the kitchen are addicted to them!

      1   cup butter, softened
    1/2   cup sugar
      1   egg
      1   teaspoon vanilla extract
  2-1/4   cups all-purpose flour
    1/2   teaspoon baking powder
    1/4   teaspoon salt
    1/2   cup raspberry jam
GLAZE:
      1   cup confectioners' sugar
      2   tablespoons evaporated milk
    1/2   teaspoon vanilla extract

In a bowl, cream butter and sugar until light and fluffy. Beat in egg and vanilla. Combine the flour, baking powder and salt; gradually add to creamed mixture and mix well.

Divide the dough into four portions; shape each into a 10-in. x 2-1/2-in. log. Place 4 in. apart on greased or foil-lined baking sheets. Make a 1/2-in. depression down the center of each log. Bake at 350° for 10 minutes.

Fill depressions with jam. Bake 10-15 minutes longer or

CHOCOLATE-DIPPED SPRITZ

NOEL COOKIE GEMS

Noel Cookie Gems

❄️ **Patsy Noel, Exeter, California**

I whip up a batch of these cookies bearing my family's namesake every Christmas. They're a cinch to assemble and freeze, saving time during the holiday rush, and they can be filled with different flavors of jam for variety.

1/4	cup butter, softened
1/4	cup shortening
3/4	cup sugar
1	egg
1	teaspoon vanilla extract
2-2/3	cups all-purpose flour
1/2	teaspoon salt
1/4	teaspoon baking powder
1/4	teaspoon baking soda
1/2	cup sour cream
3/4	cup finely chopped nuts
1/3	cup seedless strawberry jam

In a large bowl, cream the butter, shortening and sugar. Beat in egg and vanilla. Combine the flour, salt, baking powder and baking soda; gradually add to creamed mixture alternately with sour cream. Mix well. Shape into 1-1/4-in. balls; roll in nuts.

Place 2 in. apart on greased baking sheets. Using the end of a wooden spoon handle, make a 3/8- to 1/2-in.-deep indentation in the center of each ball. Fill with jam. Bake at 350° for 10-12 minutes or until lightly browned. Remove to wire racks.

Yield: 3 dozen.

Shortbread Ornament Cookies

❄️ **Taste of Home Test Kitchen**

These buttery shortbread cookie ornaments are almost too pretty to eat! Use cookie cutters of your choice for your own unique designs.

3	cups all-purpose flour
3/4	cup sugar
1/4	teaspoon salt
1-1/2	cups cold butter
2	tablespoons cold water
1/2	teaspoon rum extract
1/2	teaspoon almond extract

ICING:

2	cups confectioners' sugar
2	tablespoons plus 2 teaspoons milk

Food coloring of your choice

In a large bowl, combine the flour, sugar and salt; cut in butter until mixture resembles coarse crumbs. Stir in water and extracts until mixture forms a ball.

On a lightly floured surface, roll dough to 1/4-in. thickness. Cut with floured ornament-shaped cookie cutters. Place 1 in. apart on ungreased baking sheets. Cover and refrigerate for 30 minutes.

Bake at 325° for 15-18 minutes or until edges are lightly browned. Cool for 2 minutes before removing to wire racks to cool completely.

For icing, in a bowl, whisk confectioners' sugar and milk. Divide into small bowls; tint with food coloring. Gently spread over cookies. Decorate with additional colors of icing if desired.

Yield: about 3 dozen.

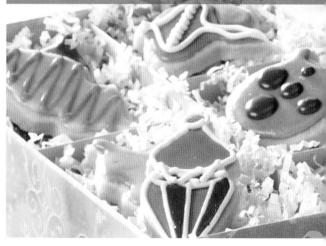
SHORTBREAD ORNAMENT COOKIES

Snowflake Cookies

❄ **Morven Baker, Ashland, Ohio**

Warm from the oven, these sweet, sugary snowflakes are guaranteed to melt in your mouth.

    2   cups butter, softened
1-1/4 cups sugar, *divided*
    1   teaspoon vanilla extract
    4   cups cake flour
    2   tablespoons edible glitter

In a large bowl, cream butter and 1 cup sugar until light and fluffy. Beat in vanilla. Gradually add flour and mix well. Divide in half. Cover and refrigerate for 2 hours or until easy to handle.

On a lightly floured surface, roll out one portion of dough to 1/4-in. thickness. Cut with a floured 4-in. snowflake-shaped cookie cutter. Place 1 in. apart on ungreased baking sheets. Bake at 325° for 7-10 minutes or until firm. Repeat with remaining dough. Chill and reroll scraps if desired.

In a small resealable plastic bag, combine edible glitter and remaining sugar. Seal bag; crush mixture to break glitter into smaller pieces. Sprinkle over warm cookies. Cool for 5 minutes before removing to wire racks to cool completely.

Yield: 4 dozen.

Editor's Note: Edible glitter is available from Wilton Industries. Call 1-800/794-5866 or visit *www.wilton.com*.

Almond Oatmeal Cutouts

❄ **Martha Dahlman, Regina, Saskatchewan**

Almond extract gives my oatmeal cookies added flavor. The dough is slightly sticky, so roll it out between sheets of waxed paper before cutting.

1/2 cup butter, softened
1/2 cup shortening
3/4 cup sugar
  2 teaspoons almond extract
1-3/4 cups all-purpose flour
1-1/4 cups old-fashioned oats

In a large bowl, cream the butter, shortening and sugar until light and fluffy. Beat in extract. Combine flour and oats; gradually add to the creamed mixture.

Roll out between waxed paper to 1/4-in. thickness. Cut with 2-1/2-in. cookie cutters dipped in flour.

Place 1 in. apart on ungreased baking sheets. Bake at 350° for 12-15 minutes or until lightly browned. Remove to wire racks to cool.

Yield: 2-1/2 dozen.

ALMOND RASPBERRY STARS

Almond Raspberry Stars

❄ **Darlene Weaver, Lebanon, Pennsylvania**

The first Christmas I tested this recipe, I quickly ended up making a second batch! Everyone enjoyed these starry delights.

3/4 cup butter, softened
1/2 cup confectioners' sugar
  1 teaspoon vanilla extract
1/2 teaspoon almond extract
1-3/4 cups plus 2 tablespoons all-purpose flour
  2 tablespoons finely chopped almonds
  1 tablespoon sugar
1/2 teaspoon ground cinnamon
  1 egg white, beaten
1/3 cup raspberry jam

In a large bowl, cream butter and confectioners' sugar until light and fluffy. Beat in extracts. Stir in flour. Shape into a ball; cover and chill for 15 minutes.

On a lightly floured surface, roll dough to 1/4-in. thickness. With floured cutters, cut dough into equal numbers of 2-1/2-in. and 1-1/2-in. stars. Combine the almonds, sugar and cinnamon. Brush small stars with egg white and immediately sprinkle with almond mixture. Leave large stars plain.

Place 1 in. apart on ungreased baking sheets. Bake small stars at 350° for 10 minutes and large stars for 12 minutes or just until the tips begin to brown. Cool on wire racks.

To assemble, spread enough jam over large star to cover the center. Top with a small star; press lightly (jam should show around edge of small star). Repeat. Let jam set before storing cookies in an airtight container.

Yield: about 3 dozen.

BUTTERSCOTCH GINGERBREAD COOKIES

Butterscotch Gingerbread Cookies

❄ Kara Cook, Elk Ridge, Utah

Every time I make these wonderful cookies, the spicy aroma takes me back to my childhood. It was Christmas tradition for my mom and I to bake and then deliver them to neighbors.

    1   cup butter, softened
    1   cup packed brown sugar
    2   eggs
    3   cups all-purpose flour
    2   packages (3-1/2 ounces *each*) cook-and-serve
        butterscotch pudding mix
    3   teaspoons ground ginger
    1   teaspoon baking powder
    1   teaspoon ground cinnamon

In a large bowl, cream the butter and brown sugar. Beat in the eggs. Combine the flour, pudding mixes, ginger, baking powder and cinnamon; gradually add to creamed mixture. Cover and refrigerate for 1 hour or until easy to handle.

On a lightly floured surface, roll out dough to 1/4-in. thickness. Cut with floured cookie cutters. Place 1 in. apart on ungreased baking sheets. Bake at 350° for 6-8 minutes or until firm. Remove to wire racks to cool. Decorate as desired.

Yield: about 2 dozen.

Orange Spritz Cookies

❄ Sean Fleming, St. Charles, Illinois

Brown sugar gives these spritz cookies a lovely light caramel tint. With a hint of orange flavor, this variation has a buttery shortbread taste with less fat than other Christmas treats. They are a delightful addition to my holiday cookie tray.

    1/2   cup butter, softened
      1   package (3 ounces) cream cheese, softened
    1/2   cup packed brown sugar
      2   teaspoons grated orange peel
    1/2   teaspoon orange *or* vanilla extract
  1-1/2   cups all-purpose flour
    1/4   teaspoon salt
Colored sugar

In a large bowl, cream the butter, cream cheese and brown sugar until light and fluffy. Beat in orange peel and extract. Combine flour and salt; gradually add to creamed mixture.

Using a cookie press fitted with the disk of your choice, press cookies 1 in. apart onto ungreased baking sheets. Sprinkle with colored sugar. Bake at 375° for 6-9 minutes or until lightly browned. Cool for 2 minutes before removing to wire racks.

Yield: about 5-1/2 dozen.

Berry Shortbread Dreams

❄ Mildred Sherrer, Fort Worth, Texas

Raspberry jam adds fruity sweetness to these rich cookies. Bake a batch or two if you're looking to include a new flavor to your holiday cookie platter.

    1   cup butter, softened
    2/3   cup sugar
    1/2   teaspoon almond extract
    2   cups all-purpose flour
    1/3   to 1/2 cup seedless raspberry jam
GLAZE:
    1   cup confectioners' sugar
    2   to 3 teaspoons water
    1/2   teaspoon almond extract

In a large bowl, cream butter and sugar until light and fluffy. Beat in extract; gradually add flour until dough forms a ball. Cover; refrigerate for 1 hour or until dough is easy to handle.

Roll into 1-in. balls. Place 1 in. apart on ungreased baking sheets. Using the end of a wooden spoon handle, make an indentation in the center. Fill with jam.

CHERRY SNOWBALLS

Bake at 350° for 14-18 minutes or until edges are lightly browned. Remove to wire racks to cool. Spoon additional jam into cookies if desired. Combine glaze ingredients; drizzle over cookies.

Yield: about 3-1/2 dozen.

Cherry Snowballs

❄ Joy Schuster, Glentana, Montana

These simple confections have a delicate flavor complemented by a cherry surprise in the center. They've become a holiday favorite in my family.

    1   cup butter, softened
    1/2 cup confectioners' sugar
    2   cups all-purpose flour
    1   jar (6 ounces) maraschino cherries without
        stems, drained and halved
Additional confectioners' sugar

In a bowl, cream butter and confectioners' sugar; gradually add flour. Shape a tablespoonful of dough around each cherry, forming a ball. Place 1 in. apart on ungreased baking sheets.

Bake at 325° for 18-20 minutes or until the bottoms are browned. Roll warm cookies in confectioners' sugar. Cool on wire racks.

Yield: about 2-1/2 dozen.

Candy Cane Cookies

❄ Pat Schmeling, Germantown, Wisconsin

I've enjoyed this cookie every holiday season since I was a child. Now my family requests this recipe before any other at Christmas.

    1/2   cup shortening
    1/2   cup butter, softened
      1   cup confectioners' sugar
      1   egg
    1-1/2 teaspoons almond extract
      1   teaspoon vanilla extract
    2-1/2 cups all-purpose flour
    1/2   teaspoon salt
    1/2   teaspoon red food coloring
    1/2   cup peppermint candy, crushed
    1/2   cup sugar

In a large bowl, cream the shortening, butter and confectioners' sugar until light and fluffy. Beat in egg and extracts. Combine flour and salt; gradually add to the creamed mixture. Divide dough in half; mix the food coloring into one half. Cover and refrigerate both doughs for 2 hours or until easy to handle.

Shape 1 teaspoon white dough into a 4-in. rope. Shape 1 teaspoon red dough into a 4-in. rope. Place ropes sided by side; press together lightly and twist. Place on ungreased baking sheet; curve top of cookie down to form handle of cane. Repeat with remaining plain and red dough, placing 2 in. apart on baking sheets.

Bake at 375° for 8-9 minutes or until set. Combine the crushed candy and sugar; sprinkle warm cookies with candy mixture. Remove to wire racks.

Yield: 4 dozen.

CANDY CANE COOKIES

CHERRY CHEESE WINDMILLS

Cherry Cheese Windmills

❄ Helen McGibbon, Downers Grove, Illinois

These pretty cookies look fancy, but are a breeze to whip up. They're perfect for the busy holiday season.

1/3	cup butter, softened
1/3	cup shortening
3/4	cup sugar
1	egg
1	tablespoon milk
1	teaspoon vanilla extract
2	cups all-purpose flour
1-1/2	teaspoons baking powder
1/4	teaspoon salt

FILLING:

1	package (3 ounces) cream cheese, softened
1/4	cup sugar
1/4	teaspoon almond extract
1/2	cup finely chopped maraschino cherries
1/4	cup sliced almonds, toasted and chopped

In a large bowl, cream the butter, shortening and sugar until light and fluffy. Beat in the egg, milk and vanilla. Combine the flour, baking powder and salt; gradually add to creamed mixture and mix well. Divide dough in half. Cover and refrigerate for 3 hours or until easy to handle.

In a small bowl, beat cream cheese, sugar and extract until smooth. Fold in cherries. On a floured surface, roll each portion of dough into a 10-in. square. With a sharp knife or pastry wheel, cut into 2-1/2-in. squares. Place 2 in. apart on ungreased baking sheets. Make 1-in. cuts from each corner toward the center of the dough.

Drop teaspoonfuls of filling in the center of each square; sprinkle with almonds. Fold alternating points to the center to form a windmill; moisten points with water and pinch gently at center to seal. Bake at 350° for 8-10 minutes or until set. Cool on wire racks.
Yield: 32 cookies.

Lemon-Butter Spritz Cookies

❄ Paula Pelis, Rocky Point, New York

I like to involve kids in the creation of these cookies, but a cookie press may be too difficult for children to master. Instead, I have them sprinkle the treats with colored sugar before baking.

2	cups butter, softened
1-1/4	cups sugar
2	eggs
	Grated peel of 1 lemon
2	teaspoons lemon juice
1	teaspoon vanilla extract
5-1/4	cups all-purpose flour
1/4	teaspoon salt
	Colored sugar

In a large bowl, cream butter and sugar. Add the eggs, lemon peel, lemon juice and vanilla; mix well. Stir together flour and salt; gradually add to creamed mixture.

Using a cookie press fitted with the disk of your choice, press dough 1 in. apart onto ungreased baking sheets. Sprinkle with colored sugar. Bake at 400° for 8-10 minutes or until lightly brown around the edges.
Yield: about 12 dozen.

LEMON-BUTTER SPRITZ COOKIES

POINSETTIA COOKIES

Bake at 350° for 7-9 minutes or until set. Remove to wire racks to cool. Combine the confectioners' sugar and milk. Pipe 1/2 teaspoon frosting in center of each cookie; top with red-hot candies.

Yield: 5 dozen.

Dipped Vanillas

❄ **Karen Bourne, Magrath, Alberta**

A touch of chocolate makes these classics stand out on a holiday cookie tray. They're a Christmas tradition in our home.

1/2	cup butter, softened
1/2	cup ground almonds
1/4	cup sugar
1	teaspoon vanilla extract
1	cup all-purpose flour
2	tablespoons cornstarch
2	squares (1 ounce *each*) semisweet chocolate
1/2	teaspoon shortening

In a small bowl, beat the butter, almonds, sugar and vanilla until blended. Gradually add flour and cornstarch; mix well. Roll into 1-in. balls; shape into crescents and place on greased baking sheets.

Bake at 375° for 8-10 minutes or until lightly browned. Cool completely on wire racks.

Melt chocolate and shortening in a microwave; stir until smooth. Dip one end of each crescent into chocolate; decorate as desired. Cool on waxed paper-lined baking sheets. Refrigerate for 30 minutes or until set.

Yield: about 2-1/2 dozen.

Poinsettia Cookies

❄ **Patricia Eckard, Singers Glen, Virginia**

I make almost 30 different kinds of cookies during the Christmas season—many to give away as gifts. These pretty pink poinsettias with a hint of cinnamon flavor are always a success!

1	cup butter, softened
1	cup confectioners' sugar
1	egg
2	to 3 drops red food coloring
2-1/3	cups all-purpose flour
3/4	teaspoon salt
1/4	cup finely crushed red-hot candies

FROSTING:

1	cup confectioners' sugar
4	teaspoons milk

Additional red-hot candies

In a large bowl, cream butter and confectioners' sugar. Beat in egg and food coloring. Combine flour and salt; gradually add to the creamed mixture. Stir in red-hots. Divide dough in half; wrap in plastic wrap. Refrigerate for at least 1 hour or until firm.

On a lightly floured surface, roll out one portion of dough into a 12-in. x 10-in. rectangle. With a sharp knife or pastry wheel, cut dough into 2-in. squares. Place 1 in. apart on lightly greased baking sheets. Cut through dough from each corner of square to within 1/2 in. of center. Fold alternating points of square to center to form a pinwheel; pinch gently at center to seal. Repeat with remaining dough.

DIPPED VANILLAS

SPICE CUTOUT COOKIES

thickness. Cut with a floured 2-in. cookie cutter. Place 1 in. apart on baking sheets coated with cooking spray. Bake at 375° for 8-10 minutes or until edges are firm. Remove to wire racks to cool.

For frosting, in a large bowl, cream butter and confectioners' sugar. Beat in vanilla and enough milk to achieve spreading consistency. Add food coloring if desired. Decorate cookies as desired.

Yield: 6 dozen.

Crispy Norwegian Bows

❄ Janie Norwood, Albany, Georgia

These delicious cookies are crispy and sweetened with a light dusting of sugar on the outside. They're a must at our house every Christmas.

    3   egg yolks
    3   tablespoons sugar
    3   tablespoons heavy whipping cream
  1/2   teaspoon ground cardamom
    1   to 1-1/4 cups all-purpose flour
Oil for deep-fat frying
Confectioners' sugar

In a large bowl, beat egg yolks and sugar until light and lemon-colored. Add cream and cardamom; mix well. Gradually add flour until dough is firm enough to roll.

On a lightly floured surface, roll into a 15-in. square. Using a pastry wheel or knife, cut into 15-in. x 1-1/2-in. strips; cut diagonally at 2-1/2-in. intervals. In the center of each diamond, make a 1-in. slit, pull one end through slit.

In an electric skillet or deep-fat fryer, heat oil to 375°. Fry bows, a few at a time, for 20-40 seconds or until golden brown on both sides. Drain on paper towels. Dust with confectioners' sugar.

Yield: 4 dozen.

Spice Cutout Cookies

❄ Lyn Chapman, Provo, Utah

With a tasty twist on gingerbread and low-fat content, these whimsical treats make a nice addition to holiday cookie platters and dessert buffets alike.

    1/4   cup butter, softened
    3/4   cup sugar
    1/4   cup prune baby food
    3/4   cup molasses
      1   egg
      3   tablespoons fat-free milk
  3-3/4   cups all-purpose flour
  1-1/2   teaspoons ground ginger
  1-1/2   teaspoons ground cinnamon
  1-1/2   teaspoons aniseed, crushed
      1   teaspoon baking soda
      1   teaspoon ground cloves
      1   teaspoon fennel seed, crushed
FROSTING:
    1/4   cup butter, softened
      5   cups confectioners' sugar
    1/2   teaspoon vanilla extract
      4   to 5 tablespoons fat-free milk
Food coloring, optional

In a large bowl, cream butter and sugar until light and fluffy. Beat in the baby food, molasses, egg and milk; mix well. Combine the flour, ginger, cinnamon, aniseed, baking soda, cloves and fennel seed; gradually add to creamed mixture. Cover and refrigerate for 2 hours or until easy to handle.

On a lightly floured surface, roll out dough to 3/16-in.

CRISPY NORWEGIAN BOWS

CARAMEL-FILLED CHOCOLATE COOKIES

Tender Italian Sugar Cookies

❄ Weda Mosellie, Phillipsburg, New Jersey

These traditional cookies are moist and tender. For added fun, tint the icing red, green and white to mimic the colors of the Italian flag.

> 3/4 cup shortening
> 3/4 cup sugar
>   3 eggs
>   1 teaspoon vanilla extract
>   3 cups all-purpose flour
>   3 teaspoons baking powder
> 1/8 teaspoon salt

ICING:

> 1/4 cup milk
>   2 tablespoons butter, melted
> 1/2 teaspoon vanilla extract
> 2-1/2 cups confectioners' sugar

Food coloring and colored sugar, optional

In a large bowl, cream shortening and sugar. Beat in eggs and vanilla. Combine the flour, baking powder and salt; gradually add to creamed mixture and mix well.

Shape dough into 1-1/2-in. balls. Place 1 in. apart on ungreased baking sheets. Bake at 400° for 8-10 minutes or until lightly browned. Remove to wire racks to cool.

For icing, in a small bowl, combine the milk, butter, vanilla and confectioners' sugar until smooth. Tint with food coloring if desired. Dip the tops of cookies in icing. Sprinkle with colored sugar if desired. Place on waxed paper until set.

Yield: 3 dozen.

Caramel-Filled Chocolate Cookies

❄ Deb Walsh, Cabery, Illinois

These yummy chocolate cookies have a creamy caramel surprise inside. With pecans on top and a contrasting white chocolate drizzle, they're almost too pretty to eat!

> 1 cup butter, softened
> 1 cup plus 1 tablespoon sugar, *divided*
> 1 cup packed brown sugar
> 2 eggs
> 1 teaspoon vanilla extract
> 2-1/2 cups all-purpose flour
> 3/4 cup baking cocoa
> 1 teaspoon baking soda
> 1-1/4 cups chopped pecans, *divided*
> 1 package (13 ounces) Rolo candies
> 4 squares (1 ounce *each*) white baking chocolate, melted

In a large bowl, cream butter, 1 cup sugar and brown sugar. Add the eggs, one at a time, beating well after each addition. Beat in vanilla. Combine the flour, cocoa and baking soda; gradually add to the creamed mixture, beating just until combined. Stir in 1/2 cup pecans.

Shape a tablespoonful of dough around each candy, forming a ball. In a small bowl, combine the remaining sugar and pecans; dip each cookie halfway. Place nut side up 2 in. apart on greased baking sheets.

Bake at 375° for 7-10 minutes or until tops are slightly cracked. Cool for 3 minutes before removing to wire racks to cool completely. Drizzle with melted white chocolate.

Yield: about 5 dozen.

TENDER ITALIAN SUGAR COOKIES

CHOCOLATE THUMBPRINT COOKIES

Chocolate Thumbprint Cookies

❄ Laura Bryant German, West Warren, Massachusetts

For a change of pace, roll the cookie dough in nonpareils instead of nuts, or top the cookies with holiday candies or peppermints instead of chocolate kisses.

```
1/2   cup butter, softened
2/3   cup sugar
  1   egg, separated
  2   tablespoons milk
  1   teaspoon vanilla extract
  1   cup all-purpose flour
1/3   cup baking cocoa
1/4   teaspoon salt
  1   cup finely chopped walnuts
FILLING:
1/2   cup confectioners' sugar
  1   tablespoon butter, softened
  2   teaspoons milk
1/4   teaspoon vanilla extract
 26   milk chocolate kisses
```

In a large bowl, cream butter and sugar until light and fluffy. Beat in the egg yolk, milk and vanilla. Combine the flour, cocoa and salt; gradually add to creamed mixture and mix well. Cover and refrigerate for 1 hour or until easy to handle.

In a small bowl, whisk egg white until foamy. Shape dough into 1-in. balls; dip in egg white, then roll in nuts. Place on greased baking sheets. Using a wooden spoon handle, make an indentation in center of each cookie. Bake at 350° for 10-12 minutes or until center is set.

For filling, combine the confectioners' sugar, butter, milk and vanilla; stir until smooth. Spoon 1/4 teaspoon into each warm cookie; gently press a chocolate kiss in the center. Carefully remove from pans to wire racks to cool.
Yield: 2 dozen.

Vanilla Butter Rollouts

❄ Colleen Sickman, Charles City, Iowa

The dough in this recipe is easy to work with after a quick 30 minutes of chilling, and the finished cookies can be decorated in a variety of festive ways.

```
1-1/2   cups butter, softened
1-1/2   cups sugar
    2   eggs
    1   tablespoon vanilla extract
    4   cups all-purpose flour
    1   teaspoon baking soda
    1   teaspoon cream of tartar
    1   teaspoon salt
```

In a large bowl, cream butter and sugar until light and fluffy. Add eggs, one at a time, beating well after each addition. Beat in vanilla. Combine the flour, baking soda, cream of tartar and salt; gradually add to the creamed mixture. Cover and refrigerate for 30 minutes or until easy to handle.

On a lightly floured surface, roll out dough to 1/4-in. thickness. Cut with lightly floured 2-1/2-in. cookie cutters. Place 2 in. apart on ungreased baking sheets.

Bake at 350° for 8-10 minutes or until edges are lightly browned. Cool for 1 minute before removing to wire racks to cool completely. Decorate as desired.
Yield: about 7 dozen.

VANILLA BUTTER ROLLOUTS

SANDWICH & SPECIALTY COOKIES 2

Delight friends and family with these rich-tasting homemade delights. The sandwich and specialty cookies offered here are loaded with melt-in-your-mouth appeal and are sure to be a hit at holiday celebrations.

CHOCOLATE LINZER COOKIES

Chocolate Linzer Cookies

❄ **Heather Peters, North Pole, Alaska**

Living in a town called North Pole, it's no surprise I love Christmas baking! My mom and I made these chocolate cookies every year while I was growing up. Now I bake them for my own family because the sweet aroma reminds me of home.

3/4	cup butter, softened
1	cup sugar
2	eggs
1/2	teaspoon almond extract
2-1/3	cups all-purpose flour
1	teaspoon baking powder
1/2	teaspoon salt
1/2	teaspoon ground cinnamon
1	cup (6 ounces) semisweet chocolate chips, melted
	Confectioners' sugar
6	tablespoons seedless raspberry jam

In a small bowl, cream butter and sugar. Add eggs, one at a time, beating well after each addition. Beat in extract. Combine the flour, baking powder, salt and cinnamon; gradually add to creamed mixture and mix well. Refrigerate for 1 hour or until easy to handle.

Divide dough in half. On a lightly floured surface, roll out one portion to 1/8-in. thickness; cut with a 2-1/2-in. round cookie cutter. Roll out remaining dough; cut with a 2-1/2-in. doughnut cutter so the center is cut out of each cookie.

Place 1 in. apart on ungreased baking sheets. Bake at 350° for 8-10 minutes or until edges are lightly browned. Remove to wire racks to cool.

Spread melted chocolate over the bottom of solid cookies. Place cookies with cutout centers over chocolate. Sprinkle with confectioners' sugar. Spoon 1/2 teaspoon jam in center of each cookie.
Yield: 2 dozen.

Cream Cheese Cookie Cups

❄ **Rachel Blackston, Mauk, Georgia**

If you're looking for a quick and easy Christmas dessert, try these yummy cookie bites. For a pretty look, use an icing bag to pipe the filling into the cups, then top each with mini chocolate candies.

1	tube (18 ounces) refrigerated chocolate chip cookie dough
4	ounces cream cheese, softened
2	tablespoons butter, softened
1/2	teaspoon vanilla extract
1-1/4	cups confectioners' sugar

Cut cookie dough in half (save one portion for another use). With floured hands, press about 1 tablespoon of dough onto the bottom and up the sides of 12 ungreased miniature muffin cups. Bake at 350° for 8-10 minutes or until lightly browned.

Using the end of a wooden spoon handle, reshape the puffed cookie cups. Cool for 5 minutes before removing from pan to a wire rack to cool completely.

In a small bowl, beat the cream cheese, butter and vanilla until smooth. Gradually beat in confectioners' sugar. Spoon into cookie cups. Store in the refrigerator.
Yield: 1 dozen.

CREAM CHEESE COOKIE CUPS

HOLIDAY SANDWICH COOKIES

In a bowl, cream butter and sugar. Add syrup; mix well. Combine flour and baking soda; gradually add to creamed mixture. Divide dough into eight portions. Roll each portion into a 9-in. log.

Place 3 in. apart on ungreased baking sheets. Bake at 300° for 25 minutes or until lightly browned. Cut into 1-in. slices. Remove to wire racks to cool. Dust cookies with confectioners' sugar.

Yield: about 6 dozen.

Holiday Sandwich Cookies

❄ Darcie Cross, Novi, Michigan

Chocolate lovers will fall for these mouth-watering sandwich cookies sure to delight. Use this recipe the next time you'd like to involve your kids or grandkids in an afternoon of cookie-decorating fun.

   6 ounces white *or* chocolate candy coating
 50 to 55 cream-filled chocolate sandwich cookies
Christmas-shaped sprinkles, snowflake decors and red and green sprinkles

In a microwave-safe bowl or heavy saucepan, melt 2 oz. of candy coating at a time, stirring until smooth. Spread melted coating over cookie tops; decorate immediately. Place on waxed paper to harden.

Yield: 50-55 cookies.

Swedish Butter Cookies

❄ Sue Soderland, Elgin, Illinois

It's impossible to eat just one of these treats. Naturally, they're a favorite with my Swedish husband and children—but anyone with a sweet tooth will appreciate them. My recipe is "well-traveled" among our friends and neighbors.

  1 cup butter, softened
  1 cup sugar
  2 teaspoons maple syrup
  2 cups all-purpose flour
  1 teaspoon baking soda
Confectioners' sugar

Chocolate Mint Wafers

❄ Michelle Kester, Cleveland, Ohio

I created these melt-in-your-mouth thin mints for a Christmas cookie exchange, and everyone raved about them. To switch up the flavor, replace the peppermint extract with almond, vanilla or another extract of your choice.

   4 ounces dark chocolate candy coating
1/8 to 1/4 teaspoon peppermint extract
 18 to 24 vanilla wafers

Place candy coating in a microwave-safe bowl. Microwave, uncovered, on high for 30-60 seconds or until smooth, stirring every 15 seconds. Stir in extract.

Dip vanilla wafers in coating; allow excess to drip off. Place on waxed paper; let stand until set. Store cookies in an airtight container.

Yield: about 1-1/2 dozen.

Editor's Note: This recipe was tested in a 1,100-watt microwave.

CHOCOLATE MINT WAFERS

RASPBERRY SANDWICH SPRITZ

Raspberry Sandwich Spritz

❄️ **Joan O'Brien, Punta Gorda, Florida**

I started baking these Christmas classics when I was a teenager, and I am still making them now for my grown children and grandkids. The combination of jam, buttery shortbread, chocolate and sprinkles adds up to a fancy and festive treat.

1	cup butter, softened
3/4	cup sugar
1	egg
1	teaspoon vanilla extract
2-1/4	cups all-purpose flour
1/2	teaspoon salt
1/4	teaspoon baking powder
1	cup seedless raspberry jam
1	cup (6 ounces) semisweet chocolate chips

Chocolate sprinkles

In a large bowl, cream butter and sugar until light and fluffy. Beat in egg and vanilla; mix well. Combine the flour, salt and baking powder; gradually add to creamed mixture.

Using a cookie press fitted with a ribbon disk, form dough into long strips on ungreased baking sheets. Cut each strip into 2-in. pieces (do not separate). Bake at 375° for 12-15 minutes or until edges are golden brown. Cut again if necessary. Remove to wire racks to cool.

Spread the bottom of half of the cookies with jam; top with remaining cookies. In a microwave, melt chocolate chips; stir until smooth. Place chocolate sprinkles on a bowl. Dip each end of cookies in melted chocolate, then in sprinkles. Place on waxed paper; let stand until firm.

Yield: 2 dozen.

Star Sandwich Cookies

❄️ **Taste of Home Test Kitchen**

These dazzling sandwich cookies are sure to be the star of your holiday dessert tray. A rich, velvety mixture of white chocolate and cream cheese forms the sweet yet simple filling.

1/2	tube refrigerated sugar cookie dough, softened
1/3	cup all-purpose flour

Red sugars, nonpareils *or* sprinkles

1	square (1 ounce) white baking chocolate
2	tablespoons cream cheese, softened
1	tablespoon butter, softened
4	drops red food coloring
1/2	cup confectioners' sugar

In a small bowl, beat cookie dough and flour until combined. Roll out on a lightly floured surface to 1/8-in. thickness. Cut with a floured 2-3/4-in. star cookie cutter. Place 2 in. apart on ungreased baking sheets.

Decorate half of the cookies with sugars, nonpareils or sprinkles. Bake at 350° for 7-9 minutes or until edges are golden brown. Remove to wire racks to cool.

In a microwave-safe bowl, melt white chocolate. Stir until smooth; cool. In a small bowl, beat the cream cheese, butter and food coloring. Gradually beat in confectioners' sugar and melted chocolate until smooth. Spread over the bottoms of plain cookies; top with decorated cookies. Store in the refrigerator.

Yield: about 1 dozen.

STAR SANDWICH COOKIES

CHOCOLATE PUDDING SANDWICHES

Chocolate Pudding Sandwiches

❄ Jan Thomas, Richmond, Virginia

These frozen sandwich delights are a favorite holiday treat and after-school snack for my kids. The inclusion of sugar-free pudding allows my diabetic husband to enjoy the cookies as well.

      1-1/2   cups cold fat-free milk
    1   package (1.4 ounces) sugar-free instant chocolate pudding mix
    1   carton (8 ounces) frozen reduced-fat whipped topping, thawed
    1   cup miniature marshmallows
    2   packages (9 ounces *each*) chocolate wafers

In a bowl, whisk milk and pudding mix for 2 minutes or until slightly thickened. Fold in whipped topping and marshmallows.

For each sandwich, spread about 2 tablespoons of pudding mixture on a chocolate wafer; top with another wafer. Stack sandwiches in an airtight container. Freeze until firm, about 3 hours. Remove cookies from the freezer 5 minutes before serving.

Yield: 43 sandwiches.

Finnish Christmas Cookies

❄ Judith Outlaw, Portland, Oregon

My friend bakes these scrumptious cookies every Christmas. They're popular at cookie exchanges, although my friend's family urges her not to trade any of them!

    2   cups butter, softened
    1   cup sugar
    4   cups all-purpose flour
    1   egg, beaten

   2/3   cup finely chopped almonds
Colored sugar, optional

In a bowl, cream butter and sugar until fluffy. Beat in flour. Cover and refrigerate for 1 hour.

Roll out onto a well-floured surface to 1/4-in. thickness. Brush lightly with egg. Sprinkle with almonds and sugar if desired. Using a fluted pastry cutter or knife, cut into 2-in. x 1-in. strips. Place 1 in. apart on ungreased baking sheets.

Bake at 350° for 10-12 minutes or until lightly browned. Cool on wire racks.

Yield: about 6 dozen.

Chocolate Caramel Wafers

❄ Susan Laubach, Vida, Montana

To keep holiday baking easy, I've come to rely on quick recipes like this one.

    1   package (14 ounces) caramels
   1/4   cup evaporated milk
    1   package (12 ounces) vanilla wafers
    8   plain milk chocolate candy bars (1.55 ounces *each*), broken into squares
Chopped pecans, optional

Place caramels and milk in a microwave-safe bowl; microwave, uncovered, on high for 2 minutes or until melted. Stir until smooth. Spread over vanilla wafers; place on ungreased baking sheets. Top each with a square of chocolate. Place in a 225° oven for 1-2 minutes or until chocolate is melted. Spread with an icing knife. Top with pecans if desired.

Yield: about 7 dozen.

Editor's Note: This recipe was tested in a 1,100-watt microwave.

CHOCOLATE CARAMEL WAFERS

CRANBERRY LEMON SANDWICHES

move to wire racks to cool.

In a bowl, combine the filling ingredients; beat until smooth. Spread on the bottoms of half of the cookies; top with remaining cookies.

Yield: about 4-1/2 dozen.

Cranberry Lemon Sandwiches

❄ **Patricia Michalski, Oswego, New York**

I bake cookies all year long, so my friends and family call me the "Cookie Lady." Whenever I bake these for Christmas, I make three batches: one to keep at home for my husband and two to give as gifts.

   1   cup butter
   1   cup shortening
   1   cup sugar
   1   cup confectioners' sugar
   2   eggs
   2   teaspoons vanilla extract
   4   cups all-purpose flour
   1   teaspoon cream of tartar
   1   teaspoon grated lemon peel
1/2   teaspoon salt
3/4   cup dried cranberries
FILLING:
2/3   cup butter, softened
2-3/4   cups confectioners' sugar
1/4   cup milk
1-1/4   teaspoons grated lemon peel

In a large bowl, cream the butter, shortening and sugars until light and fluffy. Add eggs, one at a time, beating well after each addition. Beat in vanilla. Combine the flour, cream of tartar, lemon peel and salt; gradually add to the creamed mixture and mix well. Stir in cranberries. Cover and refrigerate for 2 hours or until easy to handle.

Roll into 1-in. balls. Place 2 in. apart on ungreased baking sheets. Flatten with a glass dipped in sugar. Bake at 350° for 12-14 minutes or until edges are lightly browned. Re-

Chocolate Meringue Stars

❄ **Edna Lee, Greeley, Colorado**

These delicate, chewy cookies sure make for merry munching. Their big chocolate flavor makes it difficult to keep the kids away from them long enough for me to get them on the holiday dessert tray.

   3   egg whites
3/4   teaspoon vanilla extract
3/4   cup sugar
1/4   cup baking cocoa
GLAZE:
   3   squares (1 ounce *each*) semisweet chocolate
   1   tablespoon shortening

In a large bowl, beat egg whites and vanilla until soft peaks form. Gradually add sugar, about 2 tablespoons at a time, beating until stiff peaks form. Gently fold in cocoa.

Insert a #8b large open star tip into a pastry bag; fill half full with meringue. Pipe stars, about 1-1/4-in. diameter, or drop by rounded teaspoonfuls onto parchment paper-lined baking sheets. Bake at 300° for 30-35 minutes or until lightly browned. Remove from paper; cool on wire racks.

In a heavy saucepan or microwave, melt chocolate and shortening; stir until smooth. Dip the cookies halfway into glaze; place on waxed paper until set.

Yield: about 4 dozen.

CHOCOLATE MERINGUE STARS

RUGALACH

cookies with remaining butter; sprinkle with remaining cinnamon-sugar.

Yield: 4 dozen.

Fudge-Topped Shortbread

❄ **Valarie Wheeler, DeWitt, Michigan**

This combination of buttery shortbread and sweet chocolate is too good for words. Whenever I make this recipe, there is nothing but crumbs left. Be sure to cut these into small squares because they're very rich.

  1   cup butter, softened
1/2   cup confectioners' sugar
1/4   teaspoon salt
1-1/4   cups all-purpose flour
  1   can (14 ounces) sweetened condensed milk
  2   cups (12 ounces) semisweet chocolate chips
1/2   teaspoon almond extract
1/3   cup sliced almonds, toasted

In a bowl, cream butter, sugar and salt until fluffy. Gradually beat in flour. Spread into a greased 13-in. x 9-in. x 2-in. baking pan. Bake at 350° for 16-20 minutes or until shortbread is lightly browned.

In a microwave-safe bowl, combine condensed milk and chocolate chips. Microwave, uncovered, on high for 30-60 seconds or until chips are melted; stir until smooth. Stir in extract. Spread over the shortbread. Sprinkle with almonds and press down. Refrigerate until firm. Cut into squares.

Yield: 4 dozen.

Editor's Note: This recipe was tested in a 1,100-watt microwave.

Rugalach

❄ **Becky Phillips, Chippewa Falls, Wisconsin**

The crisp texture of these crescent-shaped cookies makes them a terrific treat to serve alongside a steaming mug of hot chocolate or coffee.

  1   cup butter, softened
  1   package (8 ounces) cream cheese, softened
  2   cups all-purpose flour
1/2   teaspoon salt
FILLING:
  1   cup sugar
  2   tablespoons ground cinnamon
1/2   cup butter, melted, *divided*
1/2   cup finely chopped pecans

In a large bowl, cream butter and cream cheese. Combine flour and salt; gradually add to the creamed mixture. Divide dough into fourths. Wrap each portion in plastic wrap; refrigerate for 1 hour or until easy to handle.

Roll out each portion between two sheets of waxed paper into a 12-in. circle. Remove top sheet of waxed paper. Combine sugar and cinnamon. Brush each circle with 1 tablespoon melted butter. Sprinkle each with 3 tablespoons cinnamon-sugar and 2 tablespoons pecans. Cut each into 12 wedges.

Roll up wedges from the wide end; place pointed side down 2 in. apart on ungreased baking sheets. Curve ends to form a crescent shape. Bake at 350° for 24-26 minutes or until golden brown. Remove to wire racks. Lightly brush warm

FUDGE-TOPPED SHORTBREAD

CHERRY KISSES

Cherry Kisses

❄ Jo Ann Blomquest, Freeport, Illinois

These yummy little kisses melt in your mouth and are practically fat-free. It's no wonder the crispy meringue morsels disappear as fast as I can whip them up.

4	egg whites
1-1/4	cups sugar
1/3	cup chopped walnuts
1/3	cup chopped pitted dates
1/3	cup chopped candied cherries

Place egg whites in a bowl; let stand at room temperature for 30 minutes. Beat on medium speed until soft peaks form. Gradually beat in sugar, 1 tablespoon at a time, on high until stiff glossy peaks form and the sugar is dissolved. Fold in the walnuts, dates and cherries.

Drop by teaspoonfuls 2 in. apart onto lightly greased baking sheets. Bake at 300° for 20-30 minutes or until lightly browned and firm to the touch. Remove to wire racks to cool. Store in an airtight container.

Yield: 6 dozen.

Cranberry Almond Biscotti

❄ Evelyn Bethards Wohlers, Columbia, Maryland

A fellow stay-at-home mom gave me this recipe so we could enjoy our latte breaks more affordably with homemade biscotti. I modified the original version by using a sugar substitute. Tangy dried cranberries and spices give it delicious flavor.

2	eggs
3	egg whites
2	tablespoons molasses
3/4	teaspoon almond extract
Sugar substitute equivalent to 1 cup sugar	
2-1/4	cups all-purpose flour
1	teaspoon baking powder
1	teaspoon ground cinnamon
1/2	teaspoon baking soda
1/2	teaspoon ground nutmeg
3/4	cup slivered almonds
1/2	cup dried cranberries
1/2	cup chopped white candy coating

In a large bowl, beat the eggs, egg whites, molasses and extract. Beat in sugar substitute. Combine the flour, baking powder, cinnamon, baking soda and nutmeg; gradually add to egg mixture (dough will be sticky).

Turn onto a floured surface. Knead in almonds and cranberries. Divide dough in half; shape each portion into a 12-in. x 3-in. rectangle. Transfer to a baking sheet coated with cooking spray.

Bake at 325° for 15-20 minutes or until lightly browned. Cool for 5 minutes. Transfer to a cutting board; with a serrated knife, cut each loaf into 16 slices. Place slices cut side down on baking sheets coated with cooking spray. Bake for 25-35 minutes or until firm, turning once. Remove to wire racks to cool.

In a microwave or heavy saucepan, melt candy coating; stir until smooth. Drizzle coating over biscotti. Store in an airtight container.

Yield: 32 cookies.

Editor's Note: This recipe was tested with Splenda No Calorie Sweetener.

CRANBERRY ALMOND BISCOTTI

RASPBERRY DREAMS

Raspberry Dreams

❄ **Lori Brown, Sioux Falls, South Dakota**

I made variations to my friend's recipe to come up with this version. Family and friends look forward to these each Christmas.

2	cups butter, softened
1	cup sugar
4	egg yolks
2	teaspoons vanilla extract
1	drop lemon juice
5-1/3	cups all-purpose flour
1/4	teaspoon salt

FILLING:

1	jar (12 ounces) raspberry preserves

ICING:

1	cup confectioners' sugar
1	drop lemon juice
1	drop red food coloring, optional
1	to 2 tablespoons milk

In a large bowl, cream butter and sugar until light and fluffy. Add egg yolks, one at a time, beating well after each addition. Beat in vanilla and lemon juice. Combine flour and salt; gradually add to the creamed mixture and mix well. Refrigerate for 1 hour or until easy to handle.

Divide dough into three portions. On a lightly floured surface, roll out each portion to 1/4-in. thickness. Cut with a 2-in. round cookie cutter. Place 1 in. apart on ungreased baking sheets.

Bake at 350° for 8-10 minutes or until edges are very lightly browned. Remove to wire racks to cool.

Spread the bottom half of the cookies with raspberry preserves; top with remaining cookies. For icing, combine the sugar, lemon juice, food coloring if desired and enough milk to achieve a drizzling consistency. Drizzle over cookies.
Yield: about 4-1/2 dozen.

Santa Claus Cookies

❄ **Mary Kaufenberg, Shakopee, Minnesota**

I only need six ingredients to create these cute Kris Kringle confections. Store-bought peanut butter sandwich cookies turn jolly with white chocolate, colored sugar, mini chips and red-hot candies.

2	packages (6 ounces *each*) white baking chocolate, chopped
1	package (1 pound) Nutter Butter sandwich cookies

Red colored sugar

32	vanilla *or* white chips
64	miniature semisweet chocolate chips
32	red-hot candies

In a heavy saucepan over low heat, melt white chocolate, stirring occasionally. Dip one end of each cookie into melted chocolate. Place on wire racks. For Santa's hat, sprinkle red sugar on top part of chocolate. Press one vanilla chip off-center on hat for pom-pom; let stand until set.

Dip other end of each cookie into melted chocolate for beard, leaving center of cookie uncovered. Place on wire racks. With a dab of melted chocolate, attach semisweet chips for eyes and a red-hot candy for nose. Place on waxed paper until chocolate sets.
Yield: 32 cookies.

SANTA CLAUS COOKIES

AUSTRIAN NUT COOKIES

Austrian Nut Cookies

❄️ **Marianne Weber, South Beach, Oregon**

These are my family's favorite Christmas cookies. For a little decorative fun, arrange the slivered almonds in a pinwheel fashion so the cookies resemble poinsettias.

        1   cup all-purpose flour
      2/3   cup finely chopped almonds
      1/3   cup sugar
      1/2   cup cold butter
      1/2   cup raspberry jam
FROSTING:
        1   square (1 ounce) unsweetened chocolate,
             melted and cooled
      1/3   cup confectioners' sugar
        2   tablespoons butter, softened
Slivered almonds

In a bowl, combine flour, chopped almonds and sugar. Cut in butter until mixture resembles coarse crumbs. Form into a ball; cover and refrigerate for 1 hour.

On a floured surface, roll the dough to 1/8-in. thickness. Cut with a 2-in. round cutter and place 1 in. apart on greased baking sheets. Bake at 375° for 7-10 minutes or until the edges are lightly browned. Remove to wire racks to cool completely. Spread 1/2 teaspoon jam on half of the cookies; top with another cookie.

For frosting, combine chocolate, confectioners' sugar and butter. Spread on tops of cookies. Decorate with slivered almonds arranged in a pinwheel.

Yield: 20 sandwich cookies.

Frosted Maple Pyramids

❄️ **Wanda Goodell, Kent, Washington**

The cute shape of these cookies makes them a splendid sight on a Christmas cookie tray. For a little variety, use star-shaped cookie cutters in place of round ones.

      1/2   cup shortening
      1/3   cup packed brown sugar
        1   egg
        1   teaspoon vanilla extract
      1/4   teaspoon maple flavoring
    1-1/4   cups all-purpose flour
      1/4   teaspoon salt
      1/4   teaspoon baking powder
FROSTING:
      1/4   cup butter, softened
      3/4   cup confectioners' sugar
        1   teaspoon vanilla extract
Red candied cherries, halved

In a large bowl, cream shortening and brown sugar. Beat in the egg, vanilla and maple flavoring. Combine the flour, salt and baking powder; gradually add to the creamed mixture. Cover and refrigerate for 2 hours or until easy to handle.

On a lightly floured surface, roll out dough to 1/8-in. thickness. With floured 2-in. round cookie cutters, cut out 18 circles. Repeat with 1-1/2-in. and 1-in. round cookie cutters. Place 1 in. apart on greased baking sheets. Bake at 375° for 7-9 minutes or until lightly browned. Remove to wire racks to cool.

In a small bowl, cream butter and confectioners' sugar. Beat in vanilla. To assemble cookies, place a 2-in. cookie on waxed paper. Spread with 1 teaspoon frosting. Top with a 1-1/2-in. cookie; frost. Garnish with candied cherries.

Yield: 1-1/2 dozen.

FROSTED MAPLE PYRAMIDS

WALNUT-FILLED PILLOWS

Chocolate-Dipped Phyllo Sticks

❄ **Taste of Home Test Kitchen**

For a little something extra-special this holiday season, make these elegant sweets created by the talented cooks in our Test Kitchen. Baked into sticks, these cookies are perfect for snacking-on-the-go.

- 4 sheets phyllo dough (14 inches x 9 inches)
- 2 tablespoons butter, melted
- 1 tablespoon sugar
- 1/4 teaspoon ground cinnamon
- 2 squares (1 ounce *each*) semisweet chocolate, finely chopped
- 1/2 teaspoon shortening
- 1/2 ounce white baking chocolate, melted

Place one sheet of phyllo dough on a work surface; brush with butter. Cover with a second sheet of phyllo; brush with butter. (Until ready to use, keep remaining phyllo covered with plastic wrap and a damp towel to prevent drying out.) Cut phyllo in half lengthwise. Cut each half into five 4-1/2-in. x 2-3/4-in. rectangles. Tightly roll each rectangle from one long side, forming a 4-1/2-in.-long stick.

Combine sugar and cinnamon. Coat sticks with cooking spray; sprinkle with cinnamon-sugar. Place on an ungreased baking sheet. Bake at 425° for 3-5 minutes or until lightly browned. Remove to a wire rack to cool. Repeat with remaining phyllo dough, butter and cinnamon-sugar.

In a microwave or small heavy saucepan, melt semisweet chocolate and shortening; stir until smooth. Dip top half of phyllo sticks in melted chocolate. Place on waxed paper; let stand until set. Drizzle with white chocolate.

Yield: 20 sticks.

Walnut-Filled Pillows

❄ **Nancy Kostrej, Canonsburg, Pennsylvania**

My tender pillow cookies, filled with a delicious walnut mixture, are my husband's favorite. He says it wouldn't be Christmas without them.

- 1/2 cup cold butter
- 1 package (3 ounces) cold cream cheese
- 1-1/4 cups all-purpose flour
- 3/4 cup ground walnuts
- 1/4 cup sugar
- 2 tablespoons milk
- 1/2 teaspoon vanilla *or* almond extract
- 1 egg, lightly beaten
- Confectioners' sugar

In a large bowl, cut butter and cream cheese into flour until mixture resembles coarse crumbs. Using your hands, blend mixture together until smooth dough forms, about 3 minutes. Pat into a rectangle; wrap in plastic wrap. Refrigerate for 1 hour or until firm. For filling, combine the walnuts, sugar, milk and vanilla.

Unwrap dough and place on a lightly floured surface. Roll into a 17-1/2-in. x 10-in. rectangle; cut into 2-1/2-in. squares. Place a level teaspoonful of filling in the center of each square. Moisten edges with water; fold in half and seal with a fork. Place 1 in. apart on ungreased baking sheets. Brush with egg.

Bake at 375° for 10-12 minutes or until edges are golden brown. Remove to wire racks to cool. Dust with confectioners' sugar.

Yield: 28 cookies.

CHOCOLATE-DIPPED PHYLLO STICKS

BUTTER BRICKLE BISCOTTI

Butter Brickle Biscotti

❄️ **Darlene Brenden, Salem, Oregon**

These twice-baked toffee cookies are a must at Christmastime. They also make great gifts.

- 1/2 cup butter, softened
- 1/2 cup sugar
- 1/4 cup packed brown sugar
- 3 eggs
- 2 teaspoons vanilla extract
- 3 cups all-purpose flour
- 2 teaspoons baking powder
- 1/4 teaspoon salt
- 1 package (7-1/2 *or* 8 ounces) English toffee bits *or* almond brickle chips

In a large bowl, cream butter and sugars until light and fluffy. Add eggs, one at a time, beating well after each addition. Beat in vanilla. Combine the flour, baking powder and salt; gradually add to creamed mixture. Stir in toffee bits.

Divide dough in half. On a parchment paper-lined baking sheet, shape each portion into a 10-in. x 2-1/2-in. rectangle. Cover and refrigerate for 30 minutes.

Bake at 350° for 30-35 minutes or until golden brown. Cool for 10 minutes. Transfer to a cutting board; cut diagonally with a serrated knife into 1/2-in. slices.

Place slices cut side down on ungreased baking sheets. Bake for 20-24 minutes or until golden brown, turning once. Remove to wire racks to cool. Store in an airtight container.

Yield: about 2-1/2 dozen.

Lemon Tea Cookies

❄️ **Phyllis Dietz, Westland, Michigan**

These sandwich cookies taste rich and buttery and have a lovely lemon filling. A Christmas tradition, the recipe has been in our family since the 1950s.

- 3/4 cup butter, softened
- 1/2 cup sugar
- 1 egg yolk
- 1/2 teaspoon vanilla extract
- 2 cups all-purpose flour
- 1/4 cup finely chopped walnuts

FILLING:
- 3 tablespoons butter, softened
- 4-1/2 teaspoons lemon juice
- 3/4 teaspoon grated orange peel
- 1-1/2 cups confectioners' sugar
- 2 drops yellow food coloring, optional

In a large bowl, cream butter and sugar until light and fluffy. Beat in the egg yolk and vanilla. Gradually add flour. Shape into two 14-in. rolls; reshape each roll into a 14-in. x 1-1/8-in. x 1-1/8-in. block. Wrap each in plastic wrap. Refrigerate dough overnight.

Unwrap and cut into 1/4-in. slices. Place 2 in. apart on ungreased baking sheets. Sprinkle half of the cookies with nuts, gently pressing into dough. Bake at 400° for 8-10 minutes or until golden brown around the edges. Remove to wire racks to cool.

In a small bowl, cream butter, lemon juice and orange peel until fluffy. Gradually add confectioners' sugar until smooth. Tint yellow if desired. Spread about 1 teaspoon on bottom of the plain cookies; place nut-topped cookies over filling.

Yield: about 4-1/2 dozen.

LEMON TEA COOKIES

BERRY-CREAM COOKIE SNAPS

Berry-Cream Cookie Snaps

❄ **Crystal Briddick, Colfax, Illinois**

My mom and I created this recipe by combining two others. These desserts are crispy on the outside and light and fluffy on the inside. A fun idea is to bake the cookies flat and serve the filling as a festive dip.

        4   ounces cream cheese, softened
    1/4   cup sugar
        2   tablespoons seedless strawberry jam
    1/4   cup heavy whipping cream, whipped
        1   to 3 drops red food coloring, optional
BATTER:
    1/2   cup sugar
    1/3   cup all-purpose flour
        2   egg whites
    1/4   teaspoon vanilla extract
    1/8   teaspoon salt
    1/4   cup butter, melted and cooled
    1/2   cup chopped fresh strawberries
Additional sugar

For filling, in a small bowl, combine cream cheese, sugar and jam until blended. Fold in whipped cream and food coloring if desired. Chill.

In a bowl, whisk the sugar, flour, egg whites, vanilla and salt until smooth. Whisk in butter until blended. Line baking sheets with parchment paper. Preparing four cookies at a time, drop batter by 1-1/2 teaspoonfuls 4 in. apart onto prepared pan. Bake at 400° for 5-8 minutes or until edges are lightly browned.

Immediately remove one cookie at a time from parchment paper and form into a tube around a greased clean round wooden clothespin. Press lightly to seal; hold until set, about

20 seconds. Remove cookie from clothespin; place on waxed paper to cool. Continue with remaining cookies. If cookies become too cool to shape, return to oven for 1 minute to soften. Repeat with remaining batter.

Just before serving, pipe or spoon filling into cookie shells. Dip end of cookie into strawberries and additional sugar. Refrigerate leftovers.

Yield: about 2 dozen.

French Christmas Cookies

❄ **Judy Wilder, Mankato, Minnesota**

Graham crackers, milk chocolate and walnuts unite in this delightfully delicious recipe. Use decorative baking cups with a holiday theme and give these cookies as gifts to family members or friends.

    1/2   cup butter, softened
        1   cup packed brown sugar
        1   cup milk
  2-3/4   cups graham cracker crumbs
        2   cups milk chocolate chips
        2   cups finely chopped walnuts
TOPPING:
  1-1/4   cups milk chocolate chips, melted

In a large bowl, cream butter and brown sugar until light and fluffy. Beat in milk. Stir in the crumbs, chips and walnuts.

Fill miniature foil baking cups three-fourths full. Place 1 in. apart on baking sheets. Bake at 375° for 10-12 minutes or until set. Cool on wire racks. Top each cookie with 1/4 teaspoon melted chocolate. Store in the refrigerator.

Yield: 9-1/2 dozen.

FRENCH CHRISTMAS COOKIES

CHRISTMAS SANDWICH COOKIES

Christmas Sandwich Cookies

❄ **Elizabeth Klager, St. Catharines, Ontario**

My mother-in-law gave me the recipe for these lovely melt-in-your-mouth cookies. They quickly became a Christmas tradition at our house.

    1   cup butter, softened
  1/2   cup confectioners' sugar
    2   teaspoons milk
    2   cups all-purpose flour
  1/2   cup cornstarch
  1/8   teaspoon salt
FILLING:
    5   tablespoons raspberry jam
FROSTING:
  1/4   cup butter, softened
    1   cup confectioners' sugar
    1   teaspoon vanilla extract
Green food coloring
Red candied cherries and colored sprinkles

In a bowl, cream butter, confectioners' sugar and milk. Combine flour, cornstarch and salt; add to the creamed mixture, beating just until dough forms a ball.

On a lightly floured surface, knead 20 times. Roll out 3/8-in. thickness. Cut with a 2-in. round cookie cutter. Place 1 in. apart on ungreased baking sheets.

Bake at 350° for 12-13 minutes or until edges are lightly browned. Remove to wire racks to cool. Spread jam over the bottom of half of the cookies; top with remaining cookies.

In a bowl, cream butter, confectioners' sugar, vanilla and food coloring. Pipe frosting in tree shapes or other decorations on cookies. Garnish with red candied cherries and colored sprinkles.

Yield: 2 dozen.

Raspberry Coconut Cookies

❄ **June Brown, Veneta, Oregon**

These rich, buttery sandwich cookies are simply divine. Raspberry preserves and a sweet cream filling make them doubly delicious.

    3/4   cup butter, softened
    1/2   cup sugar
      1   egg
      1   teaspoon vanilla extract
      2   cups all-purpose flour
    1/2   cup flaked coconut
  1-1/2   teaspoons baking powder
    1/4   teaspoon salt
FILLING:
    1/4   cup butter, softened
    3/4   cup confectioners' sugar
      2   teaspoons milk
    1/2   teaspoon vanilla extract
    1/2   cup raspberry preserves

In a large bowl, cream butter and sugar until light and fluffy. Beat in egg and vanilla. Combine the flour, coconut, baking powder and salt; gradually add to the creamed mixture and mix well.

Shape into 1-in. balls. Place 1-1/2 in. apart on ungreased baking sheets; flatten with a drinking glass dipped in flour. Bake at 350° for 12-14 minutes or until edges begin to brown. Cool on wire racks.

In a small bowl, beat the butter, confectioners' sugar, milk and vanilla until smooth. Place 1/2 teaspoon preserves and a scant teaspoon of filling on the bottom of half of the cookies; top with remaining cookies.

Yield: 2-1/2 dozen.

RASPBERRY COCONUT COOKIES

DANISH CRISPIES

Danish Crispies

❄ **Martha Nelson, Zumbrota, Minnesota**

These crispy treats are like a bread and cookie in one! Served best with a steaming cup of joe, they're a tasty addition to any holiday breakfast or brunch.

     1 package (1/4 ounce) active dry yeast
   1/2 teaspoon plus 3 tablespoons sugar, *divided*
     1 cup warm water (110° to 115°), *divided*
     3 egg yolks
     4 cups all-purpose flour
   1/3 cup nonfat dry milk powder
     1 teaspoon salt
     1 cup cold butter
FILLING:
     6 tablespoons butter, softened
   1/2 cup sugar
     1 teaspoon ground cinnamon
TOPPING:
 1-1/2 cups sugar
     1 teaspoon ground cinnamon

In a large bowl, dissolve yeast and 1/2 teaspoon sugar in 1/4 cup water; let stand for 5 minutes. Add egg yolks and remaining sugar and water; mix well.

Combine the flour, milk powder and salt; cut in butter until mixture resembles coarse crumbs. Gradually add to yeast mixture to make a soft dough. Place in a greased bowl, turning once to grease top; cover and refrigerate overnight.

Turn the dough onto a lightly floured surface. Cover with a clean kitchen towel; let rest for 10 minutes. Roll into an 18-in. x 10-in. rectangle; spread with softened butter. Combine sugar and cinnamon; sprinkle over butter. Roll up jelly-roll style, starting with a long side. Pinch edges to seal. Cut into 3/4-in. slices.

Combine topping ingredients; sprinkle some on waxed paper. Place slices, cut side down, on cinnamon-sugar; roll each into a 5-in. circle, turning to coat both sides and adding cinnamon-sugar as needed. Place 2 in. apart on greased baking sheets. Sprinkle tops with leftover cinnamon-sugar if desired. Bake at 350° for 15-20 mintes or until golden brown. Remove from pans to cool on wire racks.

Yield: about 2 dozen.

Dipped Peanut Butter Sandwich Cookies

❄ **Jackie Howell, Gordo, Alabama**

This is a tempting treat you'll love to give as gifts. The recipe is almost too simple to believe!

   1/2 cup creamy peanut butter
     1 sleeve (4 ounces) round butter-flavored crackers
     1 cup white, semisweet *or* milk chocolate chips
     1 tablespoon shortening

Spread peanut butter on half of the crackers; top with remaining crackers to make sandwiches. Refrigerate.

In a double boiler over simmering water, melt chocolate chips and shortening, stirring until smooth. Dip sandwiches and place on waxed paper until chocolate hardens.

Yield: 9 servings.

DIPPED PEANUT BUTTER SANDWICH COOKIES

CHOCOLATE-DIPPED COOKIES

Chocolate-Dipped Cookies

❄️ **Taste of Home Test Kitchen**

This tender homemade cookie from our Test Kitchen is made even better by being dipped in chocolate. The contrasting drizzle is a fancy finishing touch.

1/2	cup butter, softened
3/4	cup sugar
1	egg
1	teaspoon vanilla extract
1	cup all-purpose flour
1/3	cup baking cocoa
1/2	teaspoon baking soda
1/4	teaspoon salt
1/2	cup chopped almonds
1/2	cup miniature semisweet chocolate chips
12	ounces white candy coating disks, melted
12	ounces dark chocolate candy coating disks, melted
2	ounces milk chocolate candy coating disks, melted

In a large bowl, cream butter and sugar. Beat egg and vanilla. Combine the flour, cocoa, baking soda and salt; gradually add to the creamed mixture. Stir in almonds and chocolate chips. Cover and refrigerate for 2 hours. Divide dough in half. Shape into two 8-in. rolls; wrap each in plastic wrap. Refrigerate for 3 hours or until firm.

Unwrap and cut into 1/4-in. slices. Place 2 in. apart on greased baking sheets. Bake at 350° for 8-10 minutes or until set. Remove to wire racks to cool.

Dip half of the cookies in white coating; place on waxed paper. Dip remaining cookies in dark chocolate coating; place on waxed paper. Place milk chocolate coating in a resealable plastic bag; cut a small hole in one corner of the bag. Pipe designs on cookies. Let stand for 30 minutes or until set.

Yield: 4-1/2 dozen.

Meringue Kisses

❄️ **Tami Henke, Lockport, Illinois**

There's a tasty chocolate surprise inside these frothy kisses. They're my husband's top choice each Christmas.

3	egg whites
1/4	teaspoon cream of tartar
Pinch	salt
1	cup sugar
1	teaspoon vanilla extract

Red and green food coloring, optional

44	chocolate kisses

In a bowl, beat egg whites until foamy. Sprinkle with cream of tartar and salt; beat until soft peaks form. Gradually add sugar and vanilla, beating until stiff peaks form, about 5-8 minutes. If desired, divide batter in half and fold in red and green food coloring.

Drop by rounded tablespoonfuls 1-1/2 in. apart onto lightly greased baking sheets. Lightly press a chocolate kiss into the center of each cookie and cover it with meringue using a knife.

Bake at 275° for 30-35 minutes or until firm to the touch. Immediately remove to a wire rack to cool. Store cookies in an airtight container.

Yield: 44 cookies.

MERINGUE KISSES

DROP COOKIES

3

Simple and scrumptious, these delectable cookie classics are sure to please your palate. Whip up a batch or two in a jiffy to add to Santa's cookie platter or to enjoy with good friends over a cup of tea.

ICED CINNAMON CHIP COOKIES

Iced Cinnamon Chip Cookies

❄ Katie Jean Boyd, Roachdale, Indiana

My mom helped me bake my first batch of these special cookies when I was 8 years old. Now, I take them to gatherings and give them as gifts to friends. The cinnamon flavor and frosting make them a hit.

1	cup butter, softened
3/4	cup sugar
3/4	cup packed brown sugar
2	eggs
1	teaspoon vanilla extract
3	cups all-purpose flour
1	teaspoon baking soda
1	teaspoon salt
1	package (10 ounces) cinnamon baking chips

ICING:

1/4	cup butter, melted
1/4	cup shortening
1-1/4	cups confectioners' sugar
1	tablespoon milk
3/4	teaspoon vanilla extract

In a large bowl, cream butter and sugars. Beat in eggs and vanilla. Combine the flour, baking soda and salt; gradually add to creamed mixture and mix well. Fold in cinnamon chips.

Drop by rounded tablespoonfuls 2 in. apart onto ungreased baking sheets. Bake at 350° for 10-12 minutes or until golden brown. Remove to wire racks to cool.

In a small bowl, combine icing ingredients; beat on high speed for 1-2 minutes or until fluffy. Spread over cookies.

Yield: about 3-1/2 dozen.

Frosted Ginger Creams

❄ Shirley Clark, Columbia, Missouri

I have many recipes featuring ginger, but these soft cookies are real gems.

1/4	cup shortening
1/2	cup sugar
1	egg
1/3	cup molasses
2	cups all-purpose flour
1	teaspoon ground ginger
1/2	teaspoon baking soda
1/2	teaspoon salt
1/2	teaspoon ground cinnamon
1/2	teaspoon ground cloves
1/3	cup water

FROSTING:

1-1/2	ounces cream cheese, softened
3	tablespoons butter, softened
1	cup plus 3 tablespoons confectioners' sugar
1/2	teaspoon vanilla extract
1	to 2 teaspoons lemon juice

In a large bowl, cream shortening and sugar. Beat in egg and molasses. Combine the flour, ginger, baking soda, salt, cinnamon and cloves; gradually add to creamed mixture alternately with water (dough will be soft).

Drop by heaping teaspoonfuls 2 in. apart onto greased baking sheets. Bake at 400° for 7-8 minutes or until tops are cracked. Remove to wire racks to cool.

In a small bowl, beat cream cheese, butter and confectioners' sugar until light and fluffy. Beat in vanilla and enough lemon juice to achieve spreading consistency. Frost cookies. Store in the refrigerator.

Yield: about 4 dozen.

FROSTED GINGER CREAMS

DEVIL'S FOOD COOKIES

In a bowl, combine the cake mix, egg and whipped topping until well combined. Place confectioners' sugar in a shallow dish.

Drop dough by tablespoonfuls into sugar; turn to coat. Place 2 in. apart on greased baking sheets. Bake at 350° for 10-12 minutes or until lightly browned around the edges. Remove to wire racks to cool.

Yield: about 5 dozen.

Apple Doodles

❄ **Cecilia Lorraine Ruiz, Sunnyvale, California**

This originally started as an apple cake recipe, but I worked the ingredients into cookies and have been making them this way ever since. They make nice snacks featuring fall's delicious produce.

2/3	cup butter-flavored shortening
1	cup sugar
1	egg
1	teaspoon vanilla extract
2	cups all-purpose flour
2-1/4	teaspoons ground cinnamon
1	teaspoon baking powder
1	teaspoon baking soda
1/2	teaspoon salt
1	cup finely diced peeled tart apple
3/4	cup chopped walnuts, optional

In a large bowl, cream shortening and sugar until light and fluffy. Beat in egg and vanilla. Combine the flour, cinnamon, baking powder, baking soda and salt; stir half into the creamed mixture. Stir in the apple, walnuts if desired, and remaining dry ingredients.

Drop by heaping teaspoonfuls 3 in. apart onto lightly greased baking sheets. Bake at 375° for 13-15 minutes or until golden brown. Remove to wire racks to cool.

Yield: 3-1/2 dozen.

Devil's Food Cookies

❄ **Melanie Van Den Brink, Rock Rapids, Iowa**

These cookies taste so good you'll be surprised at their low-fat content. You get more than 2 dozen of the treats from just one box of cake mix and four other common ingredients you're sure to have on hand.

1	package (18-1/4 ounces) devil's food cake mix
2	eggs
2	tablespoons butter, softened
3	tablespoons water
1/2	cup miniature semisweet chocolate chips

In a large bowl, combine the cake mix, eggs, butter and water (batter will be thick). Fold in chocolate chips.

Drop by tablespoonfuls 2 in. apart onto baking sheets coated with cooking spray. Bake at 350° for 10-13 minutes or until set and edges are lightly browned. Cool for 2 minutes before removing to wire racks.

Yield: 28 cookies.

Strawberry Cookies

❄ **Nancy Shelton, Boaz, Kentucky**

My family finds these fruity cookies to be a light and tasty treat. I sometimes shake things up by replacing the strawberry cake mix with a lemon-flavored mix.

1	package (18-1/4 ounces) strawberry cake mix
1	egg, lightly beaten
1	carton (8 ounces) frozen whipped topping, thawed
2	cups confectioners' sugar

APPLE DOODLES

AMISH SUGAR COOKIES

1/4 cup butter, softened
1/2 cup sugar
1 egg
1-1/2 teaspoons vanilla extract
1-1/2 squares (1-1/2 ounces *each*) unsweetened chocolate, melted and cooled
1/2 cup all-purpose flour
1/4 teaspoon baking powder
1/2 teaspoon salt
2 cups chopped walnuts *or* pecans

In a bowl, cream butter and sugar. Beat in egg and vanilla. Stir in chocolate. Combine the flour, baking powder and salt; gradually add to chocolate mixture. Stir in the nuts.

Drop by rounded teaspoonfuls 2 in. apart onto ungreased baking sheets. Bake at 350° for 10-11 minutes or until edges are firm. Remove to wire racks to cool.

Yield: about 3-1/2 dozen.

Amish Sugar Cookies

❄ Sylvia Ford, Kennett, Missouri

These easy-to-make cookies melt in your mouth. After I passed this cookie recipe to my sister, she entered her batch in a local fair and won the "Best of Show" prize!

1 cup butter, softened
1 cup vegetable oil
1 cup granulated sugar
1 cup confectioners' sugar
2 eggs
1 teaspoon vanilla
4-1/2 cups all-purpose flour
1 teaspoon baking soda
1 teaspoon cream of tartar

In large bowl, beat the butter, oil and sugars. Beat in eggs until well blended. Beat in vanilla.

In separate bowl, combine flour, baking soda and cream of tartar; add to creamed mixture, mixing well.

Drop by small teaspoonfuls on ungreased baking sheet. Bake at 375° for 8-10 minutes.

Yield: about 5 dozen cookies.

Nutty Chocolate Nuggets

❄ Joann Wolfe, Toledo, Washington

My family simply can't get enough of these chocolaty drop cookies filled with nuts. They're so quick to prepare that I can whip up several batches even during the busy holiday season.

Chocolate Chip Sprinkle Cookies

❄ Heidi Cretens, Milwaukee, Wisconsin

After some trial and error with different ingredients, I whipped up this chocolate chip cookie recipe everyone in my family adores.

2 cups butter, softened
1 cup sugar
1 cup packed brown sugar
2 eggs
1-1/2 teaspoons vanilla extract
4 cups all-purpose flour
1 teaspoon baking soda
1/2 teaspoon salt
2 cups (12 ounces) semisweet chocolate chips
1/2 cup quick-cooking oats
1/2 cup crisp rice cereal
1/2 cup colored sprinkles
1/2 cup chopped pecans

In a large bowl, cream butter and sugars until light and fluffy. Add the eggs, one at a time, beating well after each addition. Beat in vanilla. Combine the flour, baking soda and salt; gradually add to creamed mixture and mix well. Stir in remaining ingredients.

Drop by rounded tablespoonfuls 2 in. apart onto greased baking sheets. Bake at 375° for 8-10 minutes or until lightly browned. Remove to wire racks to cool.

Yield: about 7-1/2 dozen.

VANILLA CHIP MAPLE COOKIES

Vanilla Chip Maple Cookies

❄ **Debra Hogenson, Brewster, Minnesota**

As a farmer, my husband works long hours so I always have fulfilling homemade treats on hand. These cookies have a distinct maple flavor and stay moist and soft—although they're never in my cookie jar for long!

1	cup shortening
1/2	cup butter, softened
2	cups packed brown sugar
2	eggs
1	teaspoon vanilla extract
1	teaspoon maple flavoring
3	cups all-purpose flour
2	teaspoons baking soda
2	cups vanilla *or* white chips
1/2	cup chopped pecans

FROSTING:

1/4	cup butter, softened
4	cups confectioners' sugar
1	teaspoon maple flavoring
4	to 6 tablespoons milk
3-1/2	cups pecan halves

In a large bowl, cream the shortening, butter and brown sugar until light and fluffy. Add eggs, one at a time, beating well after each addition. Beat in vanilla and maple flavoring. Combine the flour and baking soda; gradually add to creamed mixture. Stir in vanilla chips and pecans.

Drop by rounded tablespoonfuls 2 in. apart onto ungreased baking sheets. Bake at 350° for 8-10 minutes or until golden brown. Cool for 2 minutes before removing to wire racks.

In a small bowl, cream butter and confectioners' sugar until light and fluffy. Beat in maple flavoring and enough milk to achieve spreading consistency. Frost cooled cookies. Top each with a pecan half.

Yield: about 7 dozen.

Cherry Chocolate Cookies

❄ **Kim Williams, Fort Wayne, Indiana**

No one can resist the chewy texture of these fudgy cookies. I always double the recipe because these delicious morsels disappear quickly around our house.

2-1/2	cups butter, softened
4	cups sugar
4	eggs
4	teaspoons vanilla extract
4	cups all-purpose flour
1-1/2	cups baking cocoa
2	teaspoons baking soda
1	teaspoon salt
1	package (12 ounces) miniature semisweet chocolate chips
1	jar (16 ounces) maraschino cherries, drained and halved

In a large bowl, cream butter and sugar. Add eggs, one at a time, beating well after each addition. Beat in vanilla. Combine the flour, cocoa, baking soda and salt; gradually add to creamed mixture. Stir in chocolate chips.

Drop by heaping tablespoonfuls 3 in. apart onto ungreased baking sheets. Top each with a cherry half. Bake at 350° for 10-12 minutes or until edges are firm. Remove to wire racks to cool.

Yield: about 6-1/2 dozen.

CHERRY CHOCOLATE COOKIES

TRIPLE-CHOCOLATE BROWNIE COOKIES

Triple-Chocolate Brownie Cookies

❄ **Linda Robinson, New Braunfels, Texas**

Our family of chocolate lovers gets excited when these cookies come out of the oven. They have the texture and taste of fudge brownies, and the chocolate chip-based drizzle make them too hard to resist.

3/4	cup butter, cubed
4	squares (1 ounce *each*) unsweetened chocolate
2	cups sugar
4	eggs
1-1/2	cups all-purpose flour
1/2	cup baking cocoa
2	teaspoons baking powder
1/2	teaspoon salt
2	cups (12 ounces) semisweet chocolate chips, *divided*
2	teaspoons shortening

In a small saucepan over low heat, melt butter and unsweetened chocolate; cool. Transfer to a large bowl; add sugar and eggs. Beat until smooth. Combine the flour, cocoa, baking powder and salt; gradually add to chocolate mixture. Stir in 1-1/2 cups chocolate chips. Cover and refrigerate for 2 hours or until easy to handle.

Drop by tablespoonfuls 2 in. apart onto greased baking sheets. Bake at 350° for 7-9 minutes or until edges are set and tops are slightly cracked. Cool for 2 minutes before removing from pans to wire racks to cool completely.

In a microwave-safe bowl, heat shortening and remaining chocolate chips on high for 1 minute or until chips are melted; stir until smooth. Drizzle in zigzag fashion over cookies. Let stand for 30 minutes or until chocolate is set. Store in an airtight container.
Yield: 6 dozen.

Gumdrop Cookies

❄ **Carolyn Stromberg, Wever, Iowa**

These fun cookies are chock-full of chewy gumdrops. Since gumdrops come in multiple colors, I vary my selections depending on the holiday. Kids get such a kick out of cookies with a candy surprise inside!

3/4	cup shortening
1	cup sugar, *divided*
1/2	teaspoon almond extract
1-3/4	cups all-purpose flour
1/2	teaspoon baking soda
1/4	teaspoon salt
1	cup chopped fruit-flavored *or* spiced gumdrops
2	egg whites

In a large bowl, cream shortening and 3/4 cup sugar. Beat in extract. Combine the flour, baking soda and salt; gradually add to creamed mixture. Stir in gumdrops.

In a small bowl, beat egg whites until soft peaks form. Gradually add remaining sugar, beating until stiff peaks form. Fold into dough.

Drop by heaping teaspoonfuls 2 in. apart onto ungreased baking sheets. Bake at 350° for 12-15 minutes or until golden brown. Cool for 1 minute before removing from pans to wire racks to cool completely.
Yield: 3-1/2 dozen.

GUMDROP COOKIES

CREAM CHEESE DELIGHTS

Cream Cheese Delights

❄ Agnes Golian, Garfield Heights, Ohio

Cheesecake lovers will fall for these bite-sized, cherry-topped delicacies. Quick and easy to make, they are the perfect treat for any social gathering.

  1/2 cup butter-flavored shortening
    1 package (3 ounces) cream cheese, softened
  1/2 cup sugar
    1 egg yolk
    1 teaspoon vanilla extract
    1 cup all-purpose flour
    1 teaspoon salt
Halved maraschino cherries *or* candied cherries

In a small bowl, cream shortening, cream cheese and sugar. Beat in egg yolk and vanilla. Combine flour and salt; gradually add to the creamed mixture.

Drop by teaspoonfuls 2 in. apart onto greased baking sheets. Top each with a cherry half. Bake at 350° for 12-15 minutes or until lightly browned. Cool for 1 minute before removing to wire racks.

Yield: 2 dozen.

Peanut Butter Chocolate Chip Cookies

❄ Jeane Squires, Houston, Texas

These moist cookies have a rich peanut flavor and with just four ingredients, the recipe couldn't be simpler.

    1 cup peanut butter
    1 cup sugar
    1 egg, lightly beaten
  1/2 cup miniature semisweet chocolate chips

In a bowl, combine peanut butter, sugar and egg (batter will be stiff). Stir in the chocolate chips. Scoop level tablespoonfuls and roll into balls. Place on ungreased baking sheets and flatten with a fork. Bake at 350° for 15-18 minutes or until browned.

Yield: 2 dozen.

Editor's Note: This recipe does not use flour.

Popcorn Cookies

❄ Leigh Anne Preston, Palmyra, Indiana

It's so much fun to surprise people with the crushed popcorn in these yummy cookies. They're definitely a distinctive item on the holiday tray.

  1/2 cup butter, softened
    1 cup sugar
    1 egg
    1 teaspoon vanilla extract
1-1/4 cups all-purpose flour
  1/2 teaspoon baking soda
Pinch salt
    2 cups popped popcorn, slightly crushed
    1 cup (6 ounces) semisweet chocolate chips
  1/2 cup chopped pecans

In a large bowl, cream butter and sugar until light and fluffy. Beat in egg and vanilla. Combine the flour, baking soda and salt; gradually add to the creamed mixture. Stir in the popcorn, chocolate chips and pecans.

Drop by tablespoonfuls 2 in. apart onto greased baking sheets. Bake at 350° for 13-14 minutes or until golden brown. Remove to wire racks to cool.

Yield: 2-1/2 dozen.

POPCORN COOKIES

WHITE CHOCOLATE PUMPKIN DREAMS

White Chocolate Pumpkin Dreams

❄️ Jean Kleckner, Seattle, Washington

Pumpkin pie fans will love these delicious pumpkin cookies dotted with white chocolate chips and chopped pecans. Drizzled with a brown sugar icing, they're simply irresistible.

1	cup butter, softened
1/2	cup sugar
1/2	cup packed brown sugar
1	egg
2	teaspoons vanilla extract
1	cup canned pumpkin
2	cups all-purpose flour
3-1/2	teaspoons pumpkin pie spice
1	teaspoon baking powder
1	teaspoon baking soda
1/4	teaspoon salt
1	package (11 ounces) vanilla *or* white chips
1	cup chopped pecans

PENUCHE FROSTING:

1/2	cup packed brown sugar
3	tablespoons butter
1/4	cup milk
1-1/2	to 2 cups confectioners' sugar

In a bowl, cream butter and sugars. Beat in egg, vanilla and pumpkin. Combine dry ingredients; gradually add to the creamed mixture. Stir in chips and pecans.

Drop by rounded teaspoonfuls 2 in. apart onto ungreased baking sheets. Bake at 350° for 12-14 minutes or until firm. Remove to wire racks to cool.

For frosting, combine brown sugar and butter in a saucepan. Bring to a boil; cook over medium heat for 1 minute or until slightly thickened. Cool for 10 minutes. Add milk; beat until smooth. Beat in enough confectioners' sugar to reach desired consistency. Frost cookies.
Yield: about 4-1/2 dozen.

Brownie Mounds

❄️ Mary Turner, Blountville, Tennessee

If you crave brownies but not the longer baking time, try these quick chocolaty cookies. I usually make them for the holidays, but they're good any time of year.

1/3	cup butter, softened
3/4	cup sugar
1/3	cup light corn syrup
1	egg
3	squares (1 ounce *each*) unsweetened chocolate, melted
1	teaspoon vanilla extract
1-2/3	cups all-purpose flour
1/2	teaspoon baking powder
1/4	teaspoon salt
1/2	cup chopped walnuts

In a large bowl, cream butter and sugar until light and fluffy. Add corn syrup and egg; beat well. Stir in chocolate and vanilla. Combine the flour, baking powder and salt; add to chocolate mixture; beat well. Stir in walnuts.

Drop by tablespoonfuls 2 in. apart onto greased baking sheets. Bake at 350° for 10-12 minutes or until edges are firm. Remove to wire racks to cool.
Yield: 3 dozen.

BROWNIE MOUNDS

BUTTER PECAN COOKIES

4-1/2 cups all-purpose flour
1 teaspoon baking soda
1 teaspoon cream of tartar
1 teaspoon salt
2 cups sliced almonds
1 package English toffee bits (10 ounces) *or* almond brickle chips (7-1/2 ounces)

In a large bowl, cream the butter, oil and sugars until light and fluffy. Add eggs, one at a time, beating well after each addition. Beat in extract. Combine the flour, baking soda, cream of tartar and salt; gradually add to the creamed mixture and mix well. Stir in almonds and toffee bits.

Drop by teaspoonfuls 2 in. apart onto ungreased baking sheets. Bake at 350° for 10-12 minutes or until golden brown. Remove to wire racks to cool.

Yield: 9 dozen.

Butter Pecan Cookies

❄ Sharon Crider, St. Robert, Missouri

I enjoy these crisp, shortbread-like cookies with a cup of coffee. They're scrumptious and so easy to make.

3/4 cup butter, softened
1 package (3.4 ounces) instant butterscotch pudding mix
1-1/4 cups all-purpose flour
1/2 cup chopped pecans

In a small bowl, cream butter and butterscotch pudding mix until smooth. Gradually beat in flour. Fold in pecans. Roll into 1-1/2-in. balls.

Place 2 in. apart on greased baking sheets; flatten to 1/2 in. with a greased glass. Bake at 375° for 10-13 minutes or until light golden brown. Remove from pans to wire racks.

Yield: about 2 dozen.

Toffee Almond Sandies

❄ Vicki Crowley, Monticello, Iowa

I knew after sampling these cookies from a friend that I had to add the recipe to my bulging files. Nothing beats the delicious combination of toffee and almond.

1 cup butter, softened
1 cup vegetable oil
1 cup sugar
1 cup confectioners' sugar
2 eggs
1 teaspoon almond extract

Stuffed Date Drops

❄ Clarice Schweitzer, Sun City, Arizona

In my recipe collection, these chewy drop cookies with date-nut centers are filed under "E" for extra-special.

12 pecans *or* walnut halves
24 pitted whole dates
2 tablespoons butter, softened
1/3 cup packed brown sugar
1 egg yolk
3/4 cup all-purpose flour
1/4 teaspoon baking powder
1/4 teaspoon baking soda
1/3 cup sour cream
BROWN BUTTER FROSTING:
2 tablespoons butter
3/4 cup confectioners' sugar
1/2 teaspoon vanilla extract
1-1/2 to 2 teaspoons milk

Cut pecan or walnut halves lengthwise; stuff into dates and set aside. In a bowl, cream butter and brown sugar. Beat in egg yolk. Combine flour, baking powder and baking soda; add to creamed mixture alternately with sour cream. Stir in stuffed dates.

Drop by tablespoonfuls with one date per cookie, onto greased baking sheets. Bake at 375° for 7-9 minutes or until golden brown. Cool on wire racks.

In a saucepan, cook butter over medium heat until golden brown, about 5 minutes. Gradually stir in sugar, vanilla and milk. Frost cookies.

Yield: 2 dozen.

CHOCOLATE MALLOW DROPS

Chocolate Mallow Drops

❄️ **Marie Hattrup, The Dalles, Oregon**

I tell people these cookies are to die for, and they are quick to agree after only one taste. The fudgy treats feature a marshmallow layer topped with a drizzle of chocolate frosting.

      1/2   cup butter, softened
        1   cup sugar
        1   egg
      1/2   cup milk
        1   teaspoon vanilla extract
    1-3/4   cups all-purpose flour
      1/2   cup baking cocoa
      1/2   teaspoon baking soda
      1/2   teaspoon salt
      1/2   cup chopped pecans
       18   to 22 large marshmallows, halved
    FROSTING:
      1/4   cup butter
        2   squares (1 ounce *each*) unsweetened chocolate
        1   square (1 ounce) semisweet chocolate
        2   cups confectioners' sugar
        3   to 6 tablespoons brewed coffee

In a large bowl, cream butter and sugar until light and fluffy. Beat in the egg, milk and vanilla until smooth. Combine the flour, cocoa, baking soda and salt; gradually add to creamed mixture. Stir in pecans.

   Drop by slightly rounded tablespoonfuls 2 in. apart onto ungreased baking sheets. Bake at 375° for 6 minutes. Press a marshmallow half, cut side down, onto each cookie. Bake 2 minutes longer or until marshmallow is softened. Remove to wire racks to cool.

   In a microwave-safe bowl, melt butter and chocolate squares; stir until smooth. Beat in confectioners' sugar. Add enough coffee to achieve spreading consistency. Transfer frosting to a pastry or plastic bag; cut a small hole in one corner of bag. Pipe over cookies.

   Yield: about 3 dozen.

Cranberry Oatmeal Cookies

❄️ **Pat Habiger, Spearville, Kansas**

Dotted with cranberries, orange peel and vanilla chips, these cookies are so colorful and fun to eat. They look lovely on a dessert tray and would be a great addition to your Christmas cookie lineup.

        1   cup butter, softened
    1-1/2   cups sugar
        2   eggs
        1   teaspoon vanilla extract
        2   cups all-purpose flour
        1   teaspoon baking powder
      1/2   teaspoon salt
      1/4   teaspoon baking soda
        2   cups quick-cooking oats
        1   cup raisins
        1   cup coarsely chopped fresh *or* frozen cranberries
        1   tablespoon grated orange peel
        1   package (12 ounces) vanilla chips

In a bowl, cream butter and sugar. Add the eggs, one at a time, beating well after each addition. Beat in vanilla. Combine flour, baking powder, salt and baking soda; add to the creamed mixture. Stir in oats, raisins, cranberries and orange peel. Stir in vanilla chips.

   Drop by rounded teaspoonfuls 2 in. apart onto greased baking sheets. Bake at 375° for 10-12 minutes or until the edges are lightly browned. Cool on wire racks.

   Yield: 6 dozen.

CRANBERRY OATMEAL COOKIES

CHOCOLATE CREATIONS

4

Creamy, gooey, yummy...these recipes will satsify the chocolate lover in everyone. You're sure to fall in love with the decadent treasures and mouth-watering morsels in the pages that follow.

MINT COOKIE CANDIES

Mint Cookie Candies

❄ Taste of Home Test Kitchen

These yummy mint-chocolate bites are so delightful, you'll find it difficult to stop at one. With a combination of sweetness and crunch, they make pretty holiday gifts with mint candies on top.

   12   ounces white candy coating, coarsely chopped
    6   teaspoons shortening, *divided*
  1/4   teaspoon green food coloring
    4   mint cream-filled chocolate sandwich cookies, crushed
    2   packages (4.67 ounces *each*) mint Andes candies

In a microwave-safe bowl, melt candy coating and 4 teaspoons shortening; stir until smooth. Stir in food coloring. Pour evenly into miniature muffin cup liners. Sprinkle with cookie crumbs.

In a microwave-safe bowl, melt mint candies and remaining shortening; stir until smooth. Pour over cookie crumbs. Let stand until set.

Yield: 4 dozen.

Mocha Nut Fudge

❄ Brandy LaFountain, Marion, Michigan

I was lucky enough to inherit my grandmother's cookbook collection along with all of her recipe notations. This fudgy candy earned high marks.

    1   cup packed brown sugar
  1/3   cup evaporated milk
    2   tablespoons light corn syrup
    1   cup (6 ounces) semisweet chocolate chips

    2   teaspoons vanilla extract
    1   teaspoon instant coffee granules
    1   cup chopped walnuts

In a heavy saucepan, combine the brown sugar, milk and corn syrup. Cook and stir over medium heat until sugar is dissolved and mixture comes to a boil; boil for 2 minutes.

Remove from the heat; stir in chocolate chips, vanilla and coffee granules with a wooden spoon. Continue stirring until mixture is smooth and thick, about 5 minutes. Stir in walnuts.

Shape into two 9-in. logs; wrap each in plastic wrap. Refrigerate for 2 hours or overnight. Unwrap and cut into slices.

Yield: 1 pound.

Pistachio Cranberry Bark

❄ Susan Wacek, Pleasanton, California

I was quick to ask for this recipe after tasting it at a holiday cookie/candy exchange. For a lovely gift, fill a plate or cup with bark, gather clear cellophane around it and tie with red and green satin ribbons.

    2   cups (12 ounces) semisweet chocolate chips
    5   ounces white candy coating, chopped
    1   cup chopped pistachios, toasted, *divided*
  3/4   cup dried cranberries, *divided*

In a microwave-safe bowl, melt chocolate chips; stir until smooth. Repeat with candy coating. Stir 3/4 cup pistachios and half of the cranberries into semisweet chocolate. Thinly spread onto a waxed paper-lined baking sheet.

Drizzle with candy coating. Cut through with a knife to swirl. Sprinkle with remaining pistachios and cranberries. Chill until firm. Break into pieces. Store in an airtight container in the refrigerator.

Yield: about 1 pound.

PISTACHIO CRANBERRY BARK

HOLIDAY TRUFFLES

Holiday Truffles

✳ Jennifer Lipp, Laurel, Nebraska

I like to lavish the chocolate lovers on my list with these sumptuous truffles. They always bring me rave reviews.

> 3 packages (12 ounces *each*) semisweet chocolate chips, *divided*
> 2-1/4 cups sweetened condensed milk, *divided*
> 1/2 teaspoon orange extract
> 1/2 teaspoon peppermint extract
> 1/2 teaspoon almond extract
> 1-1/2 pounds white candy coating, melted
> 3/4 pound dark chocolate candy coating, melted
> 1/3 cup crushed peppermint candies
> 1/2 cup ground almonds
> 1/3 cup flaked coconut
> Paste food coloring, optional

In a microwave-safe bowl, melt one package of chips. Add 3/4 cup milk; mix well. Stir in orange extract. Repeat twice, adding peppermint extract to one portion and almond extract to the other.

Cover and chill for 45 minutes or until firm enough to shape into 1-in. balls. Place on three separate waxed paper-lined baking sheets. Chill for 1-2 hours or until firm.

Dip orange-flavored truffles twice in white candy coating; place on waxed paper to harden. Dip peppermint-flavored truffles in dark chocolate coating; sprinkle with peppermint candies. Dip almond-flavored truffles in dark chocolate, then sprinkle with almonds or coconut. If desired, tint white coating with food coloring; drizzle over white truffles.

Yield: about 7 dozen.

Mint-Mallow Chocolate Cups

✳ Stephanie Klym, Belfield, North Dakota

These cute chocolate cups get gobbled up whenever I set them out. The fluffy mint filling pairs well with the sweet chocolate.

> 1 cup (6 ounces) semisweet chocolate chips
> 12 large marshmallows
> 1/4 cup milk
> 1/2 teaspoon vanilla extract
> 1/8 teaspoon peppermint extract
> 3 drops red *or* green food coloring
> Dash salt
> 1/2 cup heavy whipping cream
> 3 tablespoons crushed peppermint *and/or* spearmint candies, *divided*

In a microwave, melt chocolate chips; stir until smooth. Brush evenly on the inside of 18 foil miniature muffin cup liners. Chill until set. Add a second coat of chocolate; chill until set.

Meanwhile, in a small saucepan over medium-low heat, cook and stir marshmallows and milk until the marshmallows are melted. Remove from the heat. Stir in the extracts, food coloring and salt. Cover and refrigerate for 1 hour or until thickened.

Carefully peel liners from the chocolate cups and discard. In a large bowl, beat cream until stiff peaks form. Fold in marshmallow mixture and 2 tablespoons crushed candies. Spoon into chocolate cups. Sprinkle with remaining candies. Store in the refrigerator.

Yield: 1-1/2 dozen.

MINT-MALLOW CHOCOLATE CUPS

DANDY CARAMEL CANDIES

Dandy Caramel Candies

❄ Marlen Pierce, Welch, Texas

I've made these morsels almost every Christmas for the past 35 years. Everyone enjoys the chewy treats.

1-1/2 teaspoons plus 1 cup butter, *divided*
    1 cup sugar
    1 cup packed brown sugar
    1 cup dark corn syrup
    2 cups heavy whipping cream
3-3/4 cups chopped pecans (about 1 pound)
    1 teaspoon vanilla extract
Dark *or* milk chocolate confectionery coating, melted

Butter a 13-in. x 9-in. x 2-in. pan with 1-1/2 teaspoons butter; set aside. In a heavy saucepan, combine sugars, corn syrup, butter and cream.

Bring to a boil over medium-high heat, stirring constantly. Cook over medium heat until a candy thermometer reads 248° (firm-ball stage). Remove from the heat; stir in pecans and vanilla. Quickly spread into a buttered 13-in. x 9-in. x 2-in. baking pan. Cool.

Cut into 1-in. squares. Place on waxed paper-lined baking sheets; chill thoroughly. Dip each candy into melted confectionery coating. Return to refrigerator to harden.

Yield: about 9 dozen.

Editor's Note: Confectionery coating is found in the baking section of most grocery stores. It is sometimes labeled "candy coating" and is often sold in bulk packages of 1 to 1-1/2 pounds.

Chocolate-Coated Pretzels

❄ Virginia Chronic, Robinson, Illinois

These pretty pretzels are simple to prepare and make great gifts for the holidays. They're so tasty you won't be able to stop nibbling on them all day long!

    1 to 1-1/4 pounds white *and/or* milk chocolate candy coating
    1 package (8 ounces) miniature pretzels
Nonpareils, colored jimmies and colored sugar, optional

In a microwave, melt half of candy coating at a time. Dip pretzels in candy coating; allow excess to drip off. Place on waxed paper; let stand until almost set. Garnish as desired; let stand until set.

Yield: 5-6 dozen.

Creamy Peppermint Patties

❄ Donna Gonda, North Canton, Ohio

These smooth chocolate patties fill the bill for folks who like a little sweetness after a meal but who don't want a full serving of a rich dessert.

    1 package (8 ounces) cream cheese, softened
    1 teaspoon peppermint extract
    9 cups confectioners' sugar
3/4 cup milk chocolate chips
3/4 cup semisweet chocolate chips
    3 tablespoons shortening

In a large bowl, beat the cream cheese and extract until smooth. Gradually add confectioners' sugar, beating well.

Shape into 1-in. balls. Place on waxed paper-lined baking sheets. Flatten into patties. Cover and refrigerate for 1 hour or until chilled.

In a microwave, melt chips and shortening; stir until smooth. Cool slightly. Dip patties in melted chocolate; place on waxed paper until firm. Store in the refrigerator.

Yield: about 4 dozen.

CREAMY PEPPERMINT PATTIES

MAINE POTATO CANDY

In a microwave or heavy saucepan, melt chocolate, butter and shortening; stir until smooth. Place foil or paper miniature baking cups in a miniature muffin tin. Place 1 tablespoon of chocolate mixture in each cup.

In a microwave or saucepan, heat peanut butter until melted. Spoon into cups. Top with remaining chocolate mixture. Refrigerate for 30 minutes or until firm.

Yield: 1 dozen.

Maine Potato Candy

❄ **Barbara Allen, Chelmsford, Massachusetts**

Years ago, folks in Maine ate potatoes daily and used leftovers in bread, doughnuts and candy. The tradition carries on in these delectable bars.

> 4   cups confectioners' sugar
> 4   cups flaked coconut
> 3/4 cup cold mashed potatoes (without added milk and butter)
> 1-1/2 teaspoons vanilla extract
> 1/2 teaspoon salt
> 1   pound dark chocolate candy coating

In a large bowl, combine the first five ingredients. Line a 9-in. square pan with foil; butter the foil. Spread coconut mixture into pan. Cover and chill overnight. Cut into 2-in. x 1-in. rectangles. Cover and freeze.

In a microwave or double boiler, melt candy coating. Dip bars in coating; place on waxed paper to harden. Store in an airtight container.

Yield: 2 pounds.

Peanut Butter Chocolate Cups

❄ **Aljene Wendling, Seattle, Washington**

Kids love the combination of chocolate and peanut butter in these rich, creamy candies. They're the perfect treat for school or church Christmas celebrations.

> 1   milk chocolate candy bar (7 ounces)
> 1/4 cup butter
> 1   tablespoon shortening
> 1/4 cup creamy peanut butter

Cookies & Cream Fudge

❄ **Laura Lane, Richmond, Virginia**

I invented this confection for a bake sale at our children's school. The crunchy chunks of sandwich cookie soften a bit as the mixture mellows. It's so sweet that one pan serves a crowd.

> 16 chocolate cream-filled sandwich cookies, broken into chunks, *divided*
> 1   can (14 ounces) sweetened condensed milk
> 2   tablespoons butter
> 2-2/3 cups vanilla chips
> 1   teaspoon vanilla extract

Line an 8-in. square baking pan with aluminum foil; coat with cooking spray. Place half of the broken cookies in pan.

In a heavy saucepan, combine the milk, butter and chips; cook and stir over low heat until chips are melted. Remove from heat; stir in vanilla.

Pour over cookies in pan. Sprinkle with remaining cookies. Cover and refrigerate for at least 1 hour. Cut into squares.

Yield: 3 dozen.

COOKIES & CREAM FUDGE

CHRISTMAS EVE MICE

Christmas Eve Mice

❄ Margene Pons, West Valley City, Utah

Assembling these merry mice is so much fun that the kids will definitely want to help. My daughter gave me the recipe, along with a warning...your guests just might think these treats are too cute to eat!

24	double-stuffed cream-filled chocolate sandwich cookies
1	cup (6 ounces) semisweet chocolate chips
2	teaspoons shortening
24	red maraschino cherries with stems, well drained
24	milk chocolate kisses
48	sliced almonds
1	small tube green decorative icing gel
1	small tube red decorative icing gel

Carefully twist cookies apart; set aside the halves with cream filling. Save plain halves for another use.

In a microwave or heavy saucepan, melt chocolate chips and shortening; stir until smooth. Holding each cherry by the stem, dip in melted chocolate, then press onto the bottom of a chocolate kiss. Place on the cream filling of cookie, with cherry stem extending beyond cookie edge.

For ears, place slivered almonds between the cherry and kiss. Refrigerate until set. With green gel, pipe holly leaves on the cream. With red gel, pipe holly berries between leaves and pipe eyes on each chocolate kiss. Store in an airtight container at room temperature.

Yield: 2 dozen.

Coconut Bonbons

❄ Beverly Cray, Epping, New Hampshire

My family and friends never fail to include these chocolates on their Christmas wish list. Luckily, this recipe makes a big batch—so my supply meets the candy demand.

1/2	cup butter, softened
2	pounds confectioners' sugar
1	can (14 ounces) sweetened condensed milk
4	cups chopped pecans
1	package (10 ounces) flaked coconut
1	teaspoon vanilla extract
2	cups (12 ounces) semisweet chocolate chips
1	tablespoon shortening

In a large bowl, cream butter and sugar until light and fluffy. Add the milk, pecans, coconut and vanilla; mix well. Shape into 1-in. balls. Refrigerate for 30-45 minutes or until firm. In a heavy saucepan or microwave, melt the chips and shortening; stir until smooth. Dip balls and place on waxed paper to set. Store in an airtight container.

Yield: about 21 dozen.

Crunchy Peanut Butter Balls

❄ Janice Brightwell, Jeffersonville, Indiana

I knew these bites were going to be a big hit the first time I made them, and I've been asked for the recipe countless times since. It's quick and easy to prepare, and my husband and friends rank it as their favorite Christmas treat.

1	cup peanut butter
1	jar (7 ounces) marshmallow creme
1-1/2	cups crisp rice cereal
1-1/2	cups (9 ounces) semisweet chocolate chips
4	teaspoons shortening

In a large bowl, combine the peanut butter and marshmallow creme; add cereal and stir until well coated.

In a small microwave-safe bowl, combine chocolate chips and shortening. Microwave, uncovered, for 1-2 minutes or until chips are melted; stir until smooth.

Roll cereal mixture into 1-in. balls; dip in chocolate. Place on a waxed paper-lined pan. Refrigerate until set.

Yield: 2-1/2 dozen.

Editor's Note: Reduced-fat or generic brands of peanut butter are not recommended for this recipe.

PEANUT BUTTER TRUFFLES

1 package (10 to 12 ounces) vanilla *or* white chips *or* 1 package (11-1/2 ounces) milk chocolate chips
2 teaspoons vegetable oil
1-1/4 to 1-1/2 cups M&M's miniature baking bits *or* broken pretzel pieces

In a heavy saucepan or microwave, melt chips with oil; stir until smooth. Cool for 5 minutes. Stir in baking bits or pretzels. Spread onto a waxed paper-lined baking sheet. Refrigerate for 10 minutes. Remove from the refrigerator; break into pieces. Store in an airtight container.
Yield: about 1 pound.

Peanut Butter Truffles

❄️ Kim Barker, Richmond, Texas

Crunchy granola provides a surprising texture that brings raves when people sample these yummy peanut butter truffles.

    5 ounces white candy coating, *divided*
  2/3 cup creamy peanut butter
  1/2 cup confectioners' sugar
    1 tablespoon vanilla extract
  2/3 cup crushed granola cereal with oats and honey
    6 squares (1 ounce *each*) semisweet chocolate
    2 tablespoons shortening

In a microwave, melt 3 oz. white candy coating; stir until smooth. Stir in peanut butter until smooth. Add sugar, vanilla and cereal. Chill for 2-3 hours or until easy to handle.

Shape into 1-in. balls; set aside. Melt chocolate and shortening; dip balls and place on a wire rack over waxed paper. Let stand for 15 minutes or until set. Melt the remaining coating; cool for 5 minutes. Drizzle coating over truffles. Chill for 5-10 minutes or until set. Cover and store in the refrigerator.
Yield: 3 dozen.
Editor's Note: Reduced-fat or generic brands of peanut butter are not recommended for this recipe.

Christmas Bark Candy

❄️ Taste of Home Test Kitchen

This quick-to-fix candy is sure to please all ages when added to a homemade cookie tray. Create your own variations using different flavored chips and add-ins such as crushed candy canes, dried fruits or crunchy nuts.

Chocolate Pretzel Rings

❄️ Kim Scurio, Carol Stream, Illinois

If you like chocolate-covered pretzels, you'll love these sweet and salty snacks. I use red and green M&M's for a festive touch.

   48 to 50 pretzel rings *or* mini twists
    1 package (8 ounces) milk chocolate kisses
  1/4 cup M&M's

Place the pretzels on greased baking sheets; place a chocolate kiss in the center of each ring. Bake at 275° for 2-3 minutes or until chocolate is softened. Remove from the oven.

Place an M&M on each, pressing down slightly so warm chocolate fills the ring. Refrigerate for 5-10 minutes or until chocolate is firm. Store cookies in an airtight container at room temperature.
Yield: about 4 dozen.

CHOCOLATE PRETZEL RINGS

CHOCOLATE CHIP NOUGAT

Chocolate Chip Nougat

❄ **Sandi Friest, Paynesville, Minnesota**

This sweet, chewy nougat adds a holiday charm to Yuletide gatherings. It takes a little extra effort to prepare, but candy this festive is worth it!

1	teaspoon plus 1/4 cup butter, softened, *divided*
3	cups sugar, *divided*
2/3	cup plus 1-1/4 cups light corn syrup, *divided*
2	tablespoons water
2	egg whites
2	cups chopped walnuts
2	teaspoons vanilla extract
1	cup (6 ounces) miniature semisweet chocolate chips
2	to 3 drops *each* red *and/or* green food coloring, optional

Line a 9-in. square pan with foil; grease foil with 1 teaspoon butter and set aside. In a small heavy saucepan, combine 1 cup sugar, 2/3 cup corn syrup and water. Bring to a boil over medium heat, stirring constantly. Reduce heat to medium-low. Cook, without stirring, until a candy thermometer reads 238°.

Meanwhile, beat egg whites in a heat-proof large bowl until stiff peaks form. When the syrup reaches 238°, add it in a thin stream to egg whites, beating constantly at high speed until thick; cover and set aside.

In a large heavy saucepan, combine remaining sugar and corn syrup. Bring to a boil over medium heat, stirring constantly. Reduce heat to medium-low; cook, without stirring, until a candy thermometer reads 275° (soft-crack stage).

Meanwhile, melt remaining butter. Pour hot syrup all at once into reserved egg white mixture; mix with a wooden spoon. Stir in the walnuts, vanilla and melted butter.

Pour half of nougat mixture into prepared pan; press evenly. Sprinkle with chocolate chips. If desired, tint remaining nougat mixture with red and/or green food coloring; spread over chocolate chips. Press down evenly with buttered fingers. Let stand for several hours until set. Using foil, lift nougat into 1-in. squares.

Yield: 3 pounds.

Editor's Note: We recommend that you test your candy thermometer before each use by bringing water to a boil; the thermometer should read 212°. Adjust your recipe temperature up or down based on your test.

Bavarian Mint Fudge

❄ **Sue Tucker, Edgemoor, South Carolina**

My sister-in-law sent this chocolate candy to us one Christmas, and it's been a traditional holiday treat in our home ever since.

1-1/2	teaspoons plus 1 tablespoon butter, *divided*
2	cups (12 ounces) semisweet chocolate chips
1	package (11-1/2 ounces) milk chocolate chips
1	can (14 ounces) sweetened condensed milk
1	teaspoon peppermint extract
1	teaspoon vanilla extract

Line an 11-in. x 7-in. x 2-in. pan with foil and grease the foil with 1-1/2 teaspoons butter; set aside.

In a heavy saucepan, melt the chocolate chips and remaining butter over low heat; stir until smooth. Remove from the heat; stir in the milk and extracts until well blended. Spread into prepared pan. Refrigerate until set.

Using the foil, lift fudge out of the pan. Discard the foil; cut fudge into 1-in. squares. Store in the refrigerator.

Yield: About 2-1/2 pounds.

BAVARIAN MINT FUDGE

RASPBERRY TRUFFLES

Raspberry Truffles

❄ J. Hill, Sacramento, California

Although they look fussy, these melt-in-your-mouth delights are a cinch to make. Wherever I take them, they're a hit!

- 1/2 cup evaporated milk
- 1/4 cup sugar
- 1 package (11-1/2 ounces) milk chocolate chips
- 1/4 cup seedless raspberry preserves
- 1/2 teaspoon instant coffee granules
- 3/4 cup finely chopped almonds, toasted

In a large heavy saucepan, combine milk and sugar. Bring to a rolling boil over medium heat; boil and stir for 3 minutes. Remove from the heat; stir in chocolate chips, preserves and coffee until mixture is smooth. Chill for 1 hour.

Roll into 1-in. balls; roll in almonds. Place balls on waxed paper-lined baking sheets. Chill until firm. Cover and store in the refrigerator.

Yield: 2-1/2 dozen.

Cranberry Clusters

❄ Kari Caven, Post Falls, Idaho

These chewy and crunchy treats make a nice addition to a candy tray. I sometimes use white chocolate chips in place of semisweet and replace the cashews with macadamia nuts.

- 2 cups (12 ounces) semisweet chocolate chips
- 2/3 cup dried cranberries
- 2/3 cup cashews

In a heavy saucepan or microwave, melt the chocolate chips; stir until smooth. Stir in the cranberries and cashews. Drop by teaspoonfuls onto a waxed paper-lined baking sheet. Let stand until set. Store in an airtight container.

Yield: about 2 dozen.

Chocolate Pecan Caramels

❄ June Humphrey, Strongsville, Ohio

I haven't missed a single year making these caramels for the holidays since 1964. The toasted pecans and brown sugar are so sweet to the palate.

- 1 tablespoon plus 1 cup butter, softened, *divided*
- 1-1/2 cups coarsely chopped pecans, toasted
- 1 cup (6 ounces) semisweet chocolate chips
- 2 cups packed brown sugar
- 1 cup light corn syrup
- 1/4 cup water
- 1 can (14 ounces) sweetened condensed milk
- 2 teaspoons vanilla extract

Line a 13-in. x 9-in. x 2-in. baking pan with foil; butter the foil with 1 tablespoon butter. Sprinkle with pecans and chocolate chips; set aside.

In a heavy saucepan, melt remaining butter over medium heat. Add the brown sugar, corn syrup and water. Cook and stir until mixture comes to a boil. Stir in milk. Cook, stirring constantly, until a candy thermometer reads 248° (firm-ball stage).

Remove from heat and add vanilla. Pour into prepared pan (do not scrape saucepan). Cool completely before cutting.

Yield: about 2-1/2 pounds (about 6-3/4 dozen).

Editor's Note: We recommend that you test your candy thermometer before each use by bringing water to a boil; the thermometer should read 212°. Adjust your recipe temperature up or down based on your test.

CHOCOLATE PECAN CARAMELS

ELEGANT DIPPED CHERRIES

Melt chocolate chips and remaining shortening; stir until smooth. Drizzle over the candies. Refrigerate until firm. Store candies in an airtight container.

Yield: 1-1/2 dozen.

Coated Cookie Drops

❄ **Amanda Reid, Oakville, Iowa**

It's a good thing these no-bake drops are simple to prepare because I like to serve them throughout the year. The moist, cake-like center and sweet coating are simply to die for.

    1   package (20 ounces) chocolate cream-filled
        sandwich cookies
    1   package (8 ounces) cream cheese, softened
   15   ounces white candy coating
   12   ounces chocolate candy coating
Red *and/or* green candy coating, optional

Place the cookies in a blender or food processor; cover and process until finely crushed. In a small bowl, beat cream cheese and crushed cookies until blended. Roll into 3/4-in. balls. Cover and refrigerate for at least 1 hour.

In a small saucepan over low heat, melt white candy coating, stirring until smooth; dip half of the balls to completely coat. Melt chocolate candy coating and dip remaining balls. Place on waxed paper until hardened.

Drizzle white candies with remaining chocolate coating and chocolate candies with remaining white coating. Or melt red or green candy coating and drizzle over balls. Store in the refrigerator.

Yield: about 7-1/2 dozen.

Elegant Dipped Cherries

❄ **Sedora Brown, Waynesboro, Virginia**

These sweet maraschino cherries are wrapped in unsweetened chocolate, then dipped in melted vanilla chips. A chocolate drizzle dresses them up for serving on a festive plate of sweets.

    1   jar (10 ounces) maraschino cherries with stems,
          well drained
    3   tablespoons butter, melted
    2   tablespoons light corn syrup
    1   square (1 ounce) unsweetened chocolate
    2   teaspoons half-and-half cream
    2   cups confectioners' sugar
    1   cup vanilla *or* white chips
 2-1/2   teaspoons shortening, *divided*
   1/2   cup semisweet chocolate chips

Pat cherries dry with paper towels and set aside. In a large bowl, combine the butter, corn syrup, unsweetened chocolate and cream. Stir in the confectioners' sugar.

Knead until smooth. Roll into 18 balls; flatten each into a 2-in. circle. Wrap each circle around a cherry and lightly roll in hands. Place cherries, stem side up, in a shallow paper-lined container. Cover and freeze for at least 2 hours.

The day before serving, remove the cherries from freezer. In a microwave-safe bowl, melt vanilla chips and 1-1/2 teaspoons shortening; stir until smooth.

Holding onto the stem, dip each cherry into vanilla mixture; set on waxed paper to set.

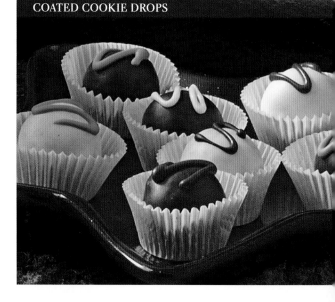

COATED COOKIE DROPS

CHOCOLATE PEPPERMINT BARK

Chocolate Peppermint Bark

❄ **Keslie Houser, Pasco, Washington**

This bark is such a snap to make, I almost feel guilty serving it...but the chocolate and mint flavors always bring guests back for more.

   6   squares (1 ounce *each*) white baking chocolate
   1   cup (6 ounces) semisweet chocolate chips
   1   cup crushed peppermint *or* spearmint candies, *divided*

In a microwave-safe bowl, melt white chocolate at 70% power; stir until smooth. Repeat with chocolate chips. Stir 6 tablespoons of crushed candies into each bowl. Drop white chocolate and semisweet chocolate in alternating spoonfuls onto a waxed paper-lined baking sheet.

   With a metal spatula, cut through chocolate to swirl, spreading to 1/4-in. thickness. Sprinkle with remaining crushed candies. Chill until firm. Break into pieces. Store in an airtight container in the refrigerator.

   Yield: about 1 pound.

   Editor's Note: This recipe was tested in a 1,100-watt microwave.

Angel Food Candy

❄ **Carrol Holloway, Hindsville, Arkansas**

Dipped in white and dark candy coatings, this two-tone treat stands out on any holiday goody tray.

1-1/2   teaspoons butter
   1   cup sugar

   1   cup dark corn syrup
   1   tablespoon white vinegar
   1   tablespoon baking soda
1/2   pound white candy coating
1/2   pound dark chocolate candy coating

Butter a 13-in. x 9-in. x 2-in. pan with 1-1/2 teaspoons butter; set aside. In a large heavy saucepan, combine the sugar, corn syrup and vinegar. Cook and stir over medium heat until sugar is dissolved. Cook, without stirring, until a candy thermometer reads 290° (soft-crack stage). Remove from the heat; stir in baking soda. Pour into the prepared pan; cool.

   Break candy into pieces. Melt white candy coating; dip the candies halfway into melted coating, shaking off excess. Place on waxed paper-lined baking sheets until set. Melt dark chocolate coating; dip uncoated portion of candies in coating. Return to waxed paper until set. Store in an airtight container.

   Yield: 1-1/2 pounds.

   Editor's Note: We recommend that you test your candy thermometer before each use by bringing water to a boil; the thermometer should read 212°. Adjust your recipe temperature up or down based on your test.

Truffle Cups

❄ **Katie Dowler, Birch Tree, Missouri**

Whenever I serve this elegant confection for the holidays, it never fails to draw compliments. Delightfully tempting, the cups are a fun, fluffy variation on traditional truffles.

   1   package (11-1/2 ounces) milk chocolate chips
   2   tablespoons shortening
   1   pound white confectionery coating, cut into 1/2-inch pieces
1/2   cup heavy whipping cream

In a double boiler or microwave, melt chips and shortening. Stir until smooth; cook for 5 minutes. With a narrow pastry brush, "paint" the chocolate mixture on the inside of 1-in. foil candy cups. Place on a tray and refrigerate until firm, about 45 minutes.

   Remove about 12 cups at a time from the refrigerator; remove and discard foil cups. Return chocolate cups to the refrigerator. For filling, melt confectionery coating and cream; stir until smooth.

   Transfer to a bowl; cover and refrigerate for 30 minutes or until mixture begins to thicken. Beat filling for 1-2 minutes or until light and fluffy. Use a pastry star tube or spoon to fill the chocolate cups. Store in the refrigerator.

   Yield: 5 dozen.

CARAMEL PRETZEL STICKS

Caramel Pretzel Sticks

❄ Mary Bown, Evanston, Wyoming

Homemade caramel, smooth almond bark and chopped nuts make these pretzel rods sinfully delicious. Your guests will think you spent all day in the kitchen!

- 2 cups sugar
- 1 cup light corn syrup
- 1 cup butter, cubed
- 1 can (14 ounces) sweetened condensed milk
- 1 package (10 ounces) pretzel rods
- 6 to 12 ounces white candy coating
- 6 to 12 ounces milk chocolate candy coating
- 3/4 cup finely chopped walnuts, optional

In a large heavy saucepan, combine the sugar, corn syrup and butter. Bring just to a boil over medium heat, stirring constantly. Continue boiling, without stirring, at a moderate-steady rate for 4 minutes. Remove from the heat; stir in milk. Return to the heat. Reduce to medium-low; cook and stir until a candy thermometer reads 245° (firm-ball stage). Keep warm.

Pour 2 cups caramel mixture into a 2-cup glass measuring cup. Quickly dip each pretzel halfway into caramel. Allow excess to drip off. Place on well-buttered baking sheets; let stand until hardened.

In a microwave-safe bowl or measuring cup, melt white candy coating. Dip half of the caramel-coated pretzels into coating. Melt milk chocolate coating; dip remaining pretzels. Drizzle white-coated pretzels with milk chocolate coating; drizzle milk chocolate-coated pretzels with white coating. Sprinkle with walnuts if desired. Store in an airtight container.

Yield: about 2-1/2 dozen.

Editor's Note: We recommend that you test your candy thermometer before each use by bringing water to a boil; the thermometer should read 212°. Adjust your recipe tem-

perature up or down based on your test. Any remaining caramel mixture may be poured into a well-buttered 8-in x 4-in. x 2-in. loaf pan. Cool to room temperature before cutting into squares and wrapping in waxed paper.

Hazelnut Toffee

❄ Joanne Simpson, Portland, Oregon

This treat is sweet and buttery with plenty of crunch. You can use dark, milk or even white chocolate and substitute almonds for the hazelnuts.

- 2 teaspoons plus 1 cup butter, *divided*
- 1 cup sugar
- 3 tablespoons water
- 1 tablespoon light corn syrup
- 1/3 cup chopped hazelnuts

TOPPING:
- 2 cups (12 ounces *each*) semisweet chocolate chips
- 1/2 cup finely chopped hazelnuts

Line a 13-in. x 9-in. x 2-in. pan with foil; coat the foil with cooking spray and set aside. Butter the sides of a large heavy saucepan with 2 teaspoons butter. Cube remaining butter; place in pan. Add the sugar, water and corn syrup. Cook and stir until mixture turns golden brown and a candy thermometer reads 300° (hard-crack stage).

Remove from the heat; stir in hazelnuts. Pour into prepared pan without scraping; spread evenly. Let stand at room temperature until cool, about 1 hour.

In a microwave-safe bowl, melt the chocolate chips. Spread over toffee; sprinkle hazelnuts. Let stand for 1 hour. Break into bite-sized pieces. Store in refrigerator.

Yield: 1-3/4 pounds.

Editor's Note: We recommend that you test your candy thermometer before each use by bringing water to a boil; the thermometer should read 212°. Adjust your recipe temperature up or down based on your test.

HAZELNUT TOFFEE

REFRIGERATOR COOKIES

5

If you have a passion for holiday baking but are short on time, you'll love the traditional slice and bake delights offered here. This chapter features a big batch of cookie-jar favorites everyone will adore.

FRUIT & NUT COOKIES

Fruit & Nut Cookies

❄ **Jennie Loftus, Gasport, New York**

I once had some fruit and nuts left over after making a fruitcake. I mixed them into a basic cookie dough along with pineapple and coconut. These soft, colorful cookies are a nice addition to a Christmas dessert tray.

3/4	cup butter, softened
3/4	cup shortening
1-1/4	cups packed brown sugar
2	eggs
1	teaspoon vanilla extract
4	cups all-purpose flour
2	teaspoons baking powder
1/2	teaspoon salt
1	can (8 ounces) crushed pineapple, drained
1/2	cup chopped dates
1/2	cup chopped red maraschino cherries
1/2	cup chopped green maraschino cherries
1/2	cup flaked coconut
1/2	cup chopped pecans *or* walnuts

In a large bowl, cream the butter, shortening and brown sugar until light and fluffy. Add eggs, one at a time, beating well after each addition. Beat in vanilla. Combine the flour, baking powder and salt; gradually add to the creamed mixture. Stir in the remaining ingredients. Shape into three 10-in. rolls; wrap each roll in plastic wrap. Refrigerate for 2 hours or until firm.

Unwrap and cut into 1/4-in. slices. Place 2 in. apart on ungreased baking sheets. Bake at 375° for 8-10 minutes or until golden brown. Remove to wire racks to cool.
Yield: 7 dozen.

Striped Icebox Cookies

❄ **Patricia Reese, Pewaukee, Wisconsin**

I've been using this recipe since I was a little girl. I like it because it's simpler than making cutout cookies. You can mix-and-match your favorite ingredients to create different looks.

1	cup butter, softened
1-1/2	cups sugar
1	egg
2-1/2	cups all-purpose flour
1-1/2	teaspoons baking powder
1/4	teaspoon salt
1/4	cup chopped maraschino cherries, drained
2	drops red food coloring
1	square (1 ounce) semisweet chocolate, melted
1	tablespoon nonpareils

In a bowl, cream butter and sugar. Beat in egg. Combine the flour, baking powder and salt; gradually add to creamed mixture. Divide into thirds; place in three bowls. Add cherries and food coloring to one portion, chocolate to another portion and nonpareils to remaining portion.

Line a 9-in. x 5-in. x 3-in. loaf pan with waxed paper. Spread cherry dough over bottom. Cover with chocolate dough, then remaining dough. Cover with plastic wrap and refrigerate for 2 hours or until firm.

Remove dough from pan; cut in half lengthwise. Cut each portion into 1/4-in. slices. Place 1 in. apart on lightly greased baking sheets. Bake at 375° for 10-12 minutes or until edges begin to brown. Remove to wire racks to cool.
Yield: 5 dozen.

STRIPED ICEBOX COOKIES

CREAM CHEESE-FILLED COOKIES

Cream Cheese-Filled Cookies

❄ **Ruth Glick, New Holland, Pennsylvania**

My aunt baked these sweet and tender treats as part of my wedding day dinner. Everyone was impressed with the cookies' eye-catching appeal and rich flavor.

- 1/3 cup butter, softened
- 1/3 cup shortening
- 3/4 cup sugar
- 1 egg
- 1 teaspoon vanilla extract
- 1-3/4 cups all-purpose flour
- 1 teaspoon baking powder
- 1/2 teaspoon salt

FILLING:
- 2 packages (3 ounces *each*) cream cheese, softened
- 1-1/2 cups confectioners' sugar
- 2 tablespoons all-purpose flour
- 1 teaspoon vanilla extract
- 1 drop yellow food coloring, optional

TOPPING:
- 3/4 cup semisweet chocolate chips
- 3 tablespoons butter

In a large bowl, cream butter, shortening and sugar. Beat in the egg and vanilla. Combine the flour, baking powder and salt; gradually add to the creamed mixture. Shape into two 12-in. rolls; wrap each roll in plastic wrap. Refrigerate for 4 hours or overnight.

Unwrap and cut into 1-in. slices. Place 1 in. apart on greased baking sheet. Bake at 375° for 10-12 minutes or until lightly browned. Immediately make an indentation in the center of each cookie using the end of a wooden spoon handle. Remove to wire racks to cool.

In a bowl, combine the filling ingredients; mix well. Place 2 teaspoonfuls in the center of each cookie. Let stand until set. In a heavy saucepan or microwave, melt chocolate chips and butter; stir until smooth. Drizzle over cookies. Store in the refrigerator.

Yield: about 2-1/2 dozen.

Snowman Sugar Cookies

❄ **Jean Wardrip Burr, Hope Mills, North Carolina**

Store-bought dough speeds up the preparation time of these cute treats. They're so easy that the whole family—even little kids—can help decorate them.

- 1 tube (18 ounces) refrigerated sugar cookie dough
- 1/2 cup shortening
- 1/2 cup butter, softened
- 4 cups confectioners' sugar
- 1 tablespoon milk
- 1 teaspoon vanilla extract
- 48 miniature semisweet chocolate chips
- 24 candy corn candies
- 1/2 cup red-hot candies

Cut cookie dough into 1/4-in. slices. Place 2 in. apart on ungreased baking sheets. Bake at 350° for 8-12 minutes or until edges are lightly browned. Cool for 2 minutes before removing to wire racks to cool completely.

For frosting, in a small bowl, cream shortening and butter. Gradually beat in confectioners' sugar. Beat in milk and vanilla until smooth. Spread over cookies. Decorate with chocolate chips, candy corn and red-hot candies.

Yield: 2 dozen.

SNOWMAN SUGAR COOKIES

PEPPERMINT CANDY COOKIES

Peppermint Candy Cookies

❄ **Gloria McKenzie, Panama City, Florida**

These mint treats with a buttery flavor practically melt in your mouth. Add bright food coloring to give them a lively look for wintertime parties.

```
1-1/4   cups butter, softened
  3/4   cup confectioners' sugar
2-1/2   cups all-purpose flour
  1/2   teaspoon salt
  1/2   teaspoon peppermint extract
```
Green and red paste *or* gel food coloring

In a large bowl, cream butter and sugar until light and fluffy. Add the flour, salt and extract; mix well. Divide dough into fourths. Tint one portion green and one red; leave the remaining portions plain.

Divide each portion into thirds; shape each into a 6-in. log. Flatten into triangular logs, bending the top of one point slightly (to give finished cookies a pinwheel effect). Assemble one large roll by alternating three green and three plain logs. Wrap in plastic wrap. Repeat with red and remaining plain dough. Refrigerate for 4 hours or until firm.

Unwrap dough and cut into 1/4-in. slices. Place 2 in. apart on ungreased baking sheets. Bake at 375° for 8-10 minutes or until edges are golden brown. Cool for 1 minute before removing to wire racks.

Cut 6-in.-square pieces of cellophane or plastic wrap to wrap each cookie; twist ends securely or tie with a ribbon.

Yield: about 4 dozen.

Double Butterscotch Cookies

❄ **Beverly Duncan, Lakeville, Ohio**

I've made this old-fashioned recipe for years. Mix up the flavor by replacing the toffee bits with miniature chocolate chips or coconut.

```
1/2   cup butter, softened
1/2   cup shortening
  4   cups packed brown sugar
  4   eggs
  1   tablespoon vanilla extract
  6   cups all-purpose flour
  3   teaspoons baking soda
  3   teaspoons cream of tartar
  1   teaspoon salt
  1   package English toffee bits (10 ounces) or
      almond brickle chips (7-1/2 ounces)
  1   cup finely chopped pecans
```

In a large bowl, cream the butter, shortening and brown sugar until light and fluffy. Add eggs, one at a time, beating well after each addition. Beat in vanilla. Combine the flour, baking soda, cream of tartar and salt; gradually add to the creamed mixture and mix well. Stir in toffee bits and pecans. Shape into three 14-in. rolls; wrap each in plastic wrap. Refrigerate for 4 hours or until firm.

Unwrap and cut into 1/2-in. slices. Place 2 in. apart on greased baking sheets. Bake at 375° for 9-11 minutes or until lightly browned. Cool for 1-2 minutes before removing from pans to wire racks to cool completely.

Yield: about 7 dozen.

DOUBLE BUTTERSCOTCH COOKIES

HOLIDAY SUGAR COOKIES

Holiday Sugar Cookies

❄ **Katie Koziolek, Hartland, Minnesota**

I add a hint of lemon to these delightful sugar cookies. For make-ahead convenience, freeze the dough up to three months, then thaw in the fridge before baking and decorating.

2	cups butter, softened
2	cups sugar
3	eggs
1	tablespoon grated lemon peel
2	teaspoons vanilla extract
6	cups all-purpose flour
1	teaspoon baking soda

FROSTING:

3	cups confectioners' sugar
3	tablespoons butter, melted
1/4	cup milk

Green food coloring
Red-hot candies

In a large bowl, cream butter and sugar. Add eggs, one at a time, beating well after each addition. Beat in lemon peel and vanilla. Combine flour and baking soda; gradually add to creamed mixture. Shape into three 10-in. rolls; wrap each in plastic wrap. Refrigerate for 4 hours or until firm.

Unwrap and cut into 1/4-in. slices. Place 2 in. apart on ungreased baking sheets. Bake at 350° for 10-15 minutes or until edges are lightly browned. Remove to wire racks.

In a bowl, combine confectioners' sugar, butter, milk and food coloring; transfer to a resealable plastic bag; drizzle over cookies in the shape of a Christmas tree. Place one red-hot candy at the top of each tree.

Yield: about 9-1/2 dozen.

Chocolate Coconut Neapolitans

❄ **Lena Marie Brownell, Rockland, Massachusetts**

These yummy striped cookies with a chocolaty twist are quick, easy and so much fun to make. The dough does requires at least 4 hours in the freezer so be sure to plan accordingly.

1	cup butter, softened
1-1/2	cups sugar
1	egg
1	teaspoon vanilla extract
2-1/2	cups all-purpose flour
1-1/2	teaspoons baking powder
1/2	teaspoon salt
1	teaspoon almond extract
4	drops red food coloring
1/2	cup flaked coconut, finely chopped
4-1/2	teaspoons chocolate syrup
1/2	cup semisweet chocolate chips
1-1/2	teaspoons shortening

Line a 9-in. x 5-in. x 3-in. loaf pan with waxed paper; set aside. In a bowl, cream butter and sugar. Beat in egg and vanilla. Combine the flour, baking powder and salt; gradually add to creamed mixture and mix well.

Divide dough into thirds. Add almond extract and red food coloring to one portion; spread evenly into prepared pan. Add coconut to second portion; spread evenly over first layer. Add chocolate syrup to third portion; spread over second layer. Cover with foil; freeze for 4 hours or overnight.

Unwrap loaf and cut in half lengthwise. Cut each portion widthwise into 1/4-in. slices. Place 2 in. apart on ungreased baking sheets. Bake at 350° for 12-14 minutes or until edges are lightly browned. Remove to wire racks to cool.

In a microwave, melt chocolate chips and shortening; stir until blended and smooth. Dip one end of each cookie into chocolate. Place on wire racks until set.

Yield: 5-1/2 dozen.

Don't Forget to Floss

Use ordinary dental floss for an easy way to slice refrigerator cookie dough. Simply slide a 1-inch piece of floss under a chilled roll of dough, crisscross the ends above the roll and pull until you've cut a perfectly round slice.

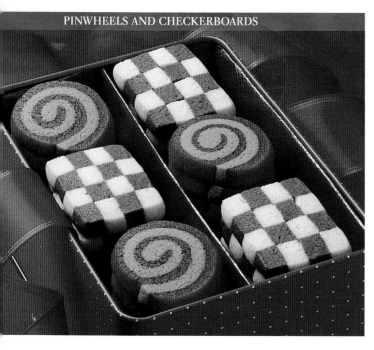

PINWHEELS AND CHECKERBOARDS

Pinwheels and Checkerboards

❄ **Jill Heatwole, Pittsville, Maryland**

My mom used to make these cookies every Christmas, and I still love them today. The dough yields two different kinds of cookies, and the colors and designs make them perfect for including in gift boxes.

1-1/4	cups butter, softened
1	cup packed brown sugar
1/2	cup sugar
2	eggs
1/4	teaspoon vanilla extract
4	cups all-purpose flour
1	teaspoon baking powder
1	teaspoon salt
1/4	teaspoon baking soda

Red and green gel food coloring
1	square (1 ounce) unsweetened chocolate, melted and cooled

In a large bowl, cream butter and sugars. Beat in eggs and vanilla. Combine flour, baking powder, salt and baking soda; gradually add to creamed mixture. Divide dough into fourths. Tint one portion red and one portion green. Stir chocolate into another portion. Wrap chocolate and plain portions in plastic wrap; chill for 1 hour or until easy to handle.

For pinwheel cookies, divide red and green portions in half. Roll out each portion between waxed paper into a 9-in. x 6-in. rectangle. Refrigerate for 30 minutes. Remove waxed paper. Place one green rectangle over a red rectangle. Roll up tightly jelly-roll style, starting with a long side; wrap in plastic wrap. Repeat. Chill for 2 hours or until firm.

For checkerboard cookies, divide plain and chocolate portions in half. Roll out each portion between waxed paper into a 6-in. x 4-in. rectangle. Cut each rectangle lengthwise into eight 1/2-in. strips. Stack the strips in groups of four, alternating plain and chocolate strips and forming eight separate stacks. Form a four-stack block by alternating chocolate-topped and plain-topped stacks. Repeat. Press together gently. Wrap in plastic. Chill for at least 2 hours.

Unwrap and cut pinwheel and checkerboard dough into 1/4-in. slices. Place 1 in. apart on ungreased baking sheets. Bake at 375° for 9-11 minutes or until set. Remove to wire racks to cool.

Yield: 6 dozen pinwheel and 4 dozen checkerboard cookies.

Orange-Pecan Icebox Cookies

❄ **Novella Cook, Hinton, West Virginia**

These crisp cookies have a zesty orange flavor and are chock-full of pecans, giving them a lightly sweet flavor. They're a perfect treat for wintertime and all year long.

1/2	cup butter, softened
1/2	cup shortening
1/2	cup sugar
1/2	cup packed brown sugar
1	egg
2	tablespoons orange juice
1	tablespoon grated orange peel
1/2	teaspoon lemon extract
1/2	teaspoon vanilla extract
2-3/4	cups all-purpose flour
1/2	teaspoon salt
1/2	teaspoon baking soda
1/4	teaspoon baking powder
1	cup finely chopped pecans

In a large bowl, cream the butter, shortening and sugars. Beat in egg, orange juice, orange peel and extracts. Combine the flour, salt, baking soda and baking powder; gradually add to the creamed mixture. Stir in pecans. Shape dough into four 5-in. rolls; wrap each in plastic wrap. Refrigerate for 3-4 hours or until firm.

Unwrap and cut into 1/4-in. slices. Place 2 in. apart on greased baking sheets. Bake at 350° for 9-10 minutes or until edges begin to brown. Remove to wire racks to cool.

Yield: about 6 dozen.

MAPLE PECAN TWISTS

Place 2 in. apart on ungreased baking sheets. Bake at 350° for 20-22 minutes or until golden brown. Remove to wire racks to cool. In a small bowl, combine icing ingredients until smooth. Drizzle over twists.

Yield: about 2 dozen.

Raspberry Nut Pinwheels

❄️ **Pat Habiger, Spearville, Kansas**

I won first prize in a recipe contest with these yummy swirl cookies. The taste of raspberry and walnuts really comes through, and they're so much fun to make!

1/2	cup butter, softened
1	cup sugar
1	egg
1	teaspoon vanilla extract
2	cups all-purpose flour
1	teaspoon baking powder
1/4	cup seedless raspberry jam
3/4	cup finely chopped walnuts

In a large bowl, cream butter and sugar until light and fluffy. Beat in egg and vanilla. Combine flour and baking powder; gradually add to creamed mixture and mix well.

Roll out dough between waxed paper into a 12-in. square. Remove top piece of waxed paper. Spread dough with jam and sprinkle with nuts. Roll up tightly jelly-roll style; wrap in plastic wrap. Refrigerate for 2 hours or until firm.

Unwrap dough and cut into 1/4-in. slices. Place 2 in. apart on ungreased baking sheets. Bake at 375° for 9-12 minutes or until edges are lightly browned. Remove to wire racks to cool.

Yield: about 3-1/2 dozen.

Maple Pecan Twists

❄️ **Doris Longman, High Springs, Florida**

These sweet treats are one of my most requested recipes for special occasions. Maple flavor is prominent in both the dough and icing of these tasty twists.

1/2	cup butter, softened
1/2	cup packed brown sugar
2	eggs
1	teaspoon maple flavoring
3	cups all-purpose flour
4	teaspoons baking powder
1/2	teaspoon salt
1/2	cup milk

FILLING:

1/4	cup butter, melted
1/2	cup finely chopped pecans

ICING:

1/4	cup butter, melted
2	cups confectioners' sugar
2	tablespoons milk
1/2	teaspoon maple flavoring

In a large bowl, cream butter and brown sugar. Add eggs, one at a time, beating well after each addition. Beat in maple flavoring. Combine the flour, baking powder and salt; add to creamed mixture alternately with milk. Cover and refrigerate for 2 hours or until easy to handle.

On a lightly floured surface, roll the dough into an 18-in. rectangle. Brush with melted butter to within 1/2 in. of edges. Sprinkle with pecans. Fold one short side of dough one third of the way over filling; fold the other short side over the top, forming an 18-in. x 3-in. rectangle. Cut into 3/4-in. strips; twist each strip twice.

RASPBERRY NUT PINWHEELS

HOLIDAY LACE COOKIES

Holiday Lace Cookies

❄ **Mildred Sherrer, Fort Worth, Texas**

It's hard to stop eating these buttery cookies dotted with pecans and dried cranberries.

1	cup butter, softened
2-1/4	cups confectioners' sugar
1/4	cup light corn syrup
1-1/4	cups all-purpose flour
1	cup chopped pecans
1/4	cup dried cranberries

In a large bowl, cream butter and confectioners' sugar. Beat in corn syrup. Gradually beat in flour. Fold in pecans and cranberries. Shape dough into two 6-in. logs; wrap each in plastic wrap. Chill for at least 2 hours or until firm.

Unwrap and cut into 1/4-in. slices. Place 3 in. apart on ungreased foil-lined baking sheets.

Bake at 350° for 11-12 minutes or until center and edges are browned and lacy. Allow cookies to cool completely before carefully removing from foil. **Yield:** 3 dozen.

Coconut Shortbread

❄ **Nancy Siefert, Wauwatosa, Wisconsin**

My family enjoys the rich flavor of these shortbread cookies so much, I bake them all year long.

2	cups butter, softened
1	cup sugar
2	teaspoons vanilla extract
4	cups all-purpose flour
1/2	cup flaked coconut

Confectioners' sugar

In a bowl, cream butter, sugar and vanilla. Gradually add flour. Stir in coconut. Shape into two 8-in. rolls; wrap each in plastic wrap. Refrigerate for 4 hours or until firm.

Unwrap and cut into 1/4-in. slices. Place 1 in. apart on ungreased baking sheets.

Bake at 350° for 12-15 minutes or until edges are lightly browned. Dip both sides of cookies in confectioners' sugar while warm. Cool on wire racks. **Yield:** 5 dozen.

Cathedral Cookies

❄ **Carol Shaffer, Cape Girardeau, Missouri**

Children love the fluffy marshmallows in these festive confections. The colorful cookies look like stained glass when sliced.

1	cup (6 ounces) semisweet chocolate chips
2	tablespoons butter
1	egg, beaten
3	cups pastel miniature marshmallows
1/2	cup chopped pecans *or* walnuts
1	cup flaked coconut

In a heavy saucepan, melt chocolate chips and butter over low heat, stirring occasionally. Stir a small amount into the egg, then return all to pan. Cook and stir over low heat for 2 minutes. Pour into a bowl; let cool for 15 minutes. Gently stir in marshmallows and nuts. Chill for 30 minutes.

Turn onto a sheet of waxed paper. Form into a roll about 1-1/2-in. diameter. Gently roll onto another sheet of waxed paper, cover the outside of the roll with the coconut. Wrap roll tightly, twisting ends to seal.

Freeze the roll for 4 hours or overnight. Remove waxed paper. Cut into 1/4-in. slices. Store in an airtight container in the refrigerator.

Yield: about 5 dozen.

CATHEDRAL COOKIES

LEMON MELTAWAYS

Lemon Meltaways

❄ Mary Houchin, Lebanon, Illinois

Both the cookie and the frosting are sparked with lemon in these melt-in-your-mouth goodies.

- 3/4 cup butter (no substitutes), softened
- 1/3 cup confectioners' sugar
- 1 teaspoon lemon juice
- 1-1/4 cups all-purpose flour
- 1/2 cup cornstarch

FROSTING:
- 1/4 cup butter, softened
- 3/4 cup confectioners' sugar
- 1 teaspoon lemon juice
- 1 teaspoon grated lemon peel
- 1 to 3 drops yellow food coloring, optional

In a bowl, cream butter and confectioners' sugar until light and fluffy; beat in lemon juice. Combine the flour and cornstarch; gradually add to the creamed mixture. Shape into two 8-in. rolls; wrap each roll in plastic wrap. Refrigerate for 2 hours or until firm.

Unwrap and cut into 1/4-inch slices. Place 2 in. apart on ungreased baking sheets. Bake at 350° for 8-12 minutes or until the cookies are firm to the touch. Remove to wire racks to cool.

For frosting, in a small bowl, combine the butter, confectioners' sugar, lemon juice, lemon peel and food coloring if desired; beat until smooth. Frost cooled cookies.

Yield: about 5 dozen.

Delicate Mint Thins

❄ Kristine McDaniel, Kettering, Ohio

Family and friends will love the fresh mint flavor of these tasty morsels. These cookies grace my holiday dessert platter every Christmas.

- 1/2 cup butter, softened
- 1/2 cup sugar
- 1 egg yolk
- 1/2 teaspoon vanilla extract
- 1-1/2 cups all-purpose flour
- 1-1/2 teaspoons baking powder
- 1/8 teaspoon salt
- 3 tablespoons milk
- 1 cup fresh mint, finely chopped
- 1-2/3 cups semisweet chocolate chips
- 1 tablespoon shortening

In a large bowl, cream butter and sugar until light and fluffy. Beat in egg yolk and vanilla. Combine the flour, baking powder and salt; add to creamed mixture alternately with milk. Stir in mint. Shape into two 8-in. rolls; wrap each in plastic wrap. Refrigerate for 2 hours or until firm.

Unwrap and cut into 1/4-in. slices. Place 1 in. apart on greased baking sheets. Bake at 350° for 8-12 minutes or until edges are golden. Remove to wire racks to cool.

In a microwave-safe bowl, melt chocolate chips and shortening; stir until smooth. Dip each cookie halfway; allowing excess to drip off. Place on waxed paper; let stand until set.

Yield: about 4-1/2 dozen.

DELICATE MINT THINS

CHOCOLATE MINT CREAMS

Chocolate Mint Creams

❄️ **Beverly Fehner, Gladstone, Missouri**

This recipe came from an old family friend and is always high on everyone's cookie request list. I make at least six batches for Noel nibbling and give some away as gifts.

    1   cup butter, softened
1-1/2   cups confectioners' sugar
    2   squares (1 ounce *each*) unsweetened chocolate, melted and cooled
    1   egg
    1   teaspoon vanilla extract
2-1/2   cups all-purpose flour
    1   teaspoon baking soda
    1   teaspoon cream of tartar
  1/4   teaspoon salt
FROSTING:
  1/4   cup butter, softened
    2   cups confectioners' sugar
    2   tablespoons milk
  1/2   teaspoon peppermint extract
Green food coloring, optional

In a large bowl, cream butter and confectioners' sugar. Add the chocolate, egg and vanilla; mix well. Combine the dry ingredients; gradually add to creamed mixture, beating well. Shape dough into a 2-in. diameter roll; wrap in plastic wrap. Refrigerate for 1 hour or until firm.

Unwrap dough and cut into 1/8-in. slices. Place 2 in. apart on ungreased baking sheets. Bake at 400° for 7-8 minutes or until edges are firm. Remove to wire racks to cool.

In a small bowl, combine frosting ingredients. Frost cookies. Store in airtight containers.

Yield: about 6 dozen.

Spiced Almond Cookies

❄️ **Wanda Daily, Milwaukie, Oregon**

These cookies are my all-time favorite! The recipe has won ribbons at fairs and applause from family and guests alike. I like it because I can freeze the dough and then whenever I need to whip up some cookies, all I have to do is remove a "log" from the freezer, thaw it and have a fresh batch in no time!

    1   cup butter, softened
  1/2   cup shortening
    1   cup packed brown sugar
    1   cup sugar
    2   eggs
    4   cups all-purpose flour
    2   teaspoons ground cinnamon
    1   teaspoon baking soda
    1   teaspoon salt
    1   teaspoon ground cloves
    1   teaspoon allspice
    1   cup slivered almonds

In a bowl, cream butter, shortening and sugars until light and fluffy. Add eggs and beat well. Combine dry ingredients; stir into creamed mixture along with nuts. Shape into three 9-in. x 1-1/2-in. rolls; wrap in plastic wrap. Refrigerate for 2-3 days for spices to blend.

Unwrap and cut into 1/4-in. slices. Place 2 in. apart on ungreased baking sheets. Bake at 350° for 12-14 minutes or until set. Remove to wire racks.

Yield: 7 dozen.

SPICED ALMOND COOKIES

SPUMONI SLICES

Peanut Chocolate Whirls

❄ **Joanne Woloschuk, Yorkton, Saskatchewan**

The mouth-watering combination of chocolate and peanut butter is irresistible in these tender swirl cookies. My daughters and I have such fun making and sharing these yummy snacks.

1/2	cup shortening
1/2	cup creamy peanut butter
1	cup sugar
1	egg
2	tablespoons milk
1	teaspoon vanilla extract
1-1/4	cups all-purpose flour
1/2	teaspoon baking soda
1/2	teaspoon salt
1	cup (6 ounces) semisweet chocolate chips

In a small bowl, cream the shortening, peanut butter and sugar. Add the egg, milk and vanilla. Combine the flour, baking soda and salt; gradually add to creamed mixture.

Cover and refrigerate for 1 hour or until easy to handle. Turn onto a lightly floured surface; roll into a 16-in. x 12-in. rectangle.

Melt chocolate chips; cool slightly. Spread over dough to within 1/2 in. of edges. Tightly roll up jelly-roll style, starting with a short side. Wrap in plastic wrap. Refrigerate for up to 30 minutes.

Unwrap and, using a serrated knife, cut into 1/4-in. slices. Place 1 in. apart on ungreased baking sheets. Bake at 350° for 8-10 minutes or until lightly browned. Remove to wire racks to cool.

Yield: about 3 dozen.

Spumoni Slices

❄ **Mary Chupp, Chattanooga, Tennessee**

These sweet rectangles get their name from the old-fashioned, tri-colored ice cream. Our whole family loves them at Christmastime and all year long.

1	cup butter, softened
1-1/2	cups confectioners' sugar
1	egg
1	teaspoon vanilla extract
2-1/2	cups all-purpose flour
2	squares (1 ounce *each*) semisweet chocolate, melted
1/2	cup chopped pecans
3	to 5 drops green food coloring
1/4	cup finely chopped candied red cherries
1/2	teaspoon almond extract
3	to 5 drops red food coloring

In a bowl, cream butter and sugar. Beat in egg and vanilla. Gradually add flour and mix well. Divide dough in three portions. Stir chocolate into one portion; mix well. Add pecans and green food coloring to the second portion. Add cherries, almond extract and red food coloring to the third.

Roll each portion between two pieces of waxed paper into an 8-in. x 6-in. rectangle. Remove waxed paper. Place chocolate rectangle on a piece of plastic wrap. Top with the green and pink rectangles; press together lightly. Wrap with plastic wrap and chill overnight.

Cut chilled dough in half lengthwise. Return one rectangle to the refrigerator. Cut remaining rectangle into 1/8-in. slices. Place 1 in. apart on ungreased baking sheets.

Bake at 375° for 5-7 minutes or until set. Cool for 2 minutes before removing to wire racks. Repeat with remaining chilled dough.

Yield: about 7 dozen.

PEANUT CHOCOLATE WHIRLS

CAPPUCCINO FLATS

Cappuccino Flats

❄️ Jacqueline Cline, Drummond, Wisconsin

These coffee-flavored cookies are so scrumptious, most people can't believe they're made in my own kitchen instead of a gourmet bakery!

1/2	cup butter, softened
1/2	cup shortening
1/2	cup sugar
1/2	cup packed brown sugar
1	tablespoon instant coffee granules
1	teaspoon warm water
1	egg
2	squares (1 ounce *each*) unsweetened chocolate, melted and cooled
2	cups all-purpose flour
1	teaspoon ground cinnamon
1/4	teaspoon salt
1-1/2	cups semisweet chocolate chips
3	tablespoons shortening

In a large bowl, cream butter, shortening and sugars until light and fluffy. Dissolve coffee in water; add to creamed mixture with egg and melted chocolate until blended. Combine flour, cinnamon and salt; gradually add to creamed mixture and mix well (dough will be sticky). Shape into two 6-1/2-in. rolls; wrap each in plastic wrap. Refrigerate for 4 hours or until firm.

Unwrap and cut into 1/4-in. slices. Place 2 in. apart on ungreased baking sheets. Bake at 350° for 10-12 minutes or until firm. Remove to wire racks to cool.

In a microwave, melt chocolate chips and shortening; stir until smooth. Dip each cookie halfway in chocolate; allow excess to drip off. Place on waxed paper; let stand until set.

Yield: 4-1/2 dozen.

Angel Wings

❄️ R. Lane, Tenafly, New Jersey

I knew I'd hit a winner with these crisp, sugar-dipped roll-ups the first time I served them after Christmas dinner. Light and buttery, they're a family favorite.

1	cup cold butter, cubed
1-1/2	cups all-purpose flour
1/2	cup sour cream
10	tablespoons sugar, *divided*
1	tablespoon ground cinnamon, *divided*

Colored sugar, optional

In a bowl, cut butter into flour until the mixture resembles coarse crumbs. Stir in the sour cream. Turn onto a lightly floured surface; knead 6-8 times or until mixture holds together. Shape into four balls; flatten slightly. Wrap in plastic wrap; refrigerate for 4 hours or overnight.

Unwrap one ball. Sprinkle 2 tablespoons sugar on waxed paper; coat all sides of ball with sugar. Roll into a 12-in. x 5-in. rectangle between two sheets of waxed paper. Remove top sheet of waxed paper. Sprinkle dough with 3/4 teaspoon cinnamon. Lightly mark a line down the center of the dough, making two 6-in. x 5-in. rectangles.

Starting with a short side, roll up jelly-roll style to the center mark; peel waxed paper away while rolling. Repeat with other short side. Wrap in plastic wrap; freeze for 30 minutes. Repeat three times. Place remaining sugar or place colored sugar if desired on waxed paper. Unwrap one roll. Cut into 1/2-in. slices; dip each side into sugar. Place 2 in. apart on ungreased baking sheets.

Bake at 375° for 12 minutes or until golden brown. Turn cookies; bake 5-8 minutes longer. Remove to wire racks to cool.

Yield: about 3 dozen.

ANGEL WINGS

CHOCOLATE CHIP ICEBOX COOKIES

Chocolate Chip Icebox Cookies

❄ **Betty Holzinger, West Olive, Michigan**

Chocolate chips make these classic refrigerator cookies absolutely delicious. This yummy treat is always welcome at our house.

3	tablespoons butter, softened
2	tablespoons shortening
1/4	cup sugar
1/4	cup packed brown sugar
1	egg yolk
1/2	teaspoon vanilla extract
2/3	cup all-purpose flour
1/4	teaspoon baking soda
1/4	teaspoon salt
1/4	cup miniature semisweet chocolate chips
1/4	cup finely chopped pecans

In a small bowl, cream the butter, shortening and sugars. Beat in egg yolk and vanilla; mix well. Combine the flour, baking soda and salt; gradually add to creamed mixture and mix well. Stir in chips and pecans. Shape into a 9-in. roll; wrap in plastic wrap. Refrigerate overnight.

Unwrap and cut into 1/4-in. slices. Place 2 in. apart on ungreased baking sheets. Bake at 375° for 8-10 minutes or until edges are golden brown. Cool for 2 minutes before removing to wire racks to cool completely.

Yield: 20 cookies.

Cranberry Slices

❄ **Stacy Duffy, Chicago, Illinois**

The cranberry and ginger in these cookies gives them a refreshing burst of flavor.

1	cup butter, softened
1/2	cup sugar
1	egg yolk
1	teaspoon vanilla extract
1/2	teaspoon salt
2-1/4	cups all-purpose flour
1/2	cup dried cranberries, chopped
6	tablespoons mined crystallized ginger, optional

In a bowl, cream butter, sugar, egg yolk, vanilla and salt until light and fluffy. Gradually add flour. Stir in cranberries and ginger if desired. Divide the dough in half; form each half into a 6-in. x 3-in. x 1-in. block. Cover with plastic wrap and refrigerate for 3 hours or up to 2 days.

To bake, cut the dough into 1/4-in. thick slices; place on ungreased parchment-lined baking sheets. Bake at 350° for 12-15 minutes or until edges are golden.

Yield: 4 dozen.

Editor's Note: Crystallized ginger is available the Asian food section in grocery stores.

Favorite Molasses Cookies

❄ **Marjorie Jenkins, Lees Summit, Missouri**

These delightful molasses cookies are chewy on the inside and crispy on the outside.

3/4	cup butter, softened
1	cup sugar
1/4	cup molasses
1	egg
2	cups all-purpose flour
2	teaspoons baking powder
1/2	teaspoon baking soda
1	teaspoon ground cinnamon
1/2	teaspoon ground cloves
1/2	teaspoon ground ginger

In a bowl, cream butter and sugar. Beat in molasses and egg. Combine dry ingredients; gradually add to creamed mixture. Chill for 1 hour or until firm.

Shape into 1-in. balls; place on greased baking sheets. Press flat with a glass dipped in sugar. Bake at 375° for 8-10 minutes or until lightly browned. Cool on wire racks.

Yield: 6 dozen.

CHERRY CRANBERRY PINWHEELS

Cherry Cranberry Pinwheels

❄️ **Deb Perry, Bluffton, Indiana**

With the combination of cranberries, cherries, orange zest and cinnamon, these colorful cookies are as fragrant as they are flavorful.

1-1/2 cups dried cranberries
    1 jar (10 ounces) cherry spreadable fruit
  1/4 cup water
  1/2 teaspoon ground cinnamon
DOUGH:
  1/4 cup butter, softened
1-1/4 cups sugar
    3 egg whites
    3 tablespoons canola oil
    2 tablespoons fat-free milk
    2 teaspoons vanilla extract
1-1/2 teaspoons grated orange peel
3-1/3 cups all-purpose flour
  3/4 teaspoon baking powder
  1/2 teaspoon ground cinnamon
  1/8 teaspoon baking soda

For filling, combine the first four ingredients in a small saucepan. Cook and stir over medium heat for 8 minutes or until liquid is absorbed and cranberries are softened. Remove from the heat; cool slightly. Transfer to a blender; cover and process until smooth. Transfer to a bowl; cover and refrigerate until chilled.

For dough, in a large bowl, beat butter and sugar for 2 minutes or until crumbly. Add egg whites, oil, milk, vanilla and orange peel; mix well. Combine the flour, baking powder, cinnamon and baking soda; gradually add to sugar mixture.

Divide dough in half. On a floured surface, roll one portion of dough into a 14-in. x 9-in. rectangle. Spread with half of the filling. Roll up jelly-roll style, starting with a long side.

Repeat with remaining dough and filling. Wrap each roll in plastic wrap; refrigerate for at least 4 hours.

Unwrap dough; cut into 1/2-in. slices. Place 2 in. apart on baking sheets coated with cooking spray. Bake at 375° for 10-12 minutes or until bottoms are lightly browned (do not overbake). Remove to wire racks to cool.

Yield: 4-1/2 to 5 dozen.

Two-Tone Butter Cookies

❄️ **Kathy Kittell, Lenexa, Kansas**

During the hectic holiday season, you'll appreciate the ease of these irresistible butter cookies. It's wonderful to pull the two-tone dough from the freezer and bake a festive batch in no time.

1 cup butter, softened
1 cup confectioners' sugar
1 teaspoon vanilla extract
2 cups all-purpose flour
Red and green liquid *or* paste food coloring
Red colored sugar, optional

In a large bowl, cream butter and confectioners' sugar. Beat in vanilla. Add flour and mix well. Divide dough in half; with food coloring, tint half red and half green. Shape each portion into an 8-in. log. Wrap in plastic wrap and refrigerate for at least 1 hour.

Cut each log in half lengthwise. Press red and green halves together. Tightly wrap each roll in plastic wrap; freeze for up to 6 months.

To prepare cookies: Let dough stand at room temperature for 15 minutes. Cut into 1/4-in. slices; place 2 in. apart on ungreased baking sheets. Sprinkle with colored sugar if desired. Bake at 350° for 12-14 minutes or until set. Cool on wire racks.

Yield: about 5 dozen.

TWO-TONE BUTTER COOKIES

BARS & BROWNIES

6

There's nothing better than biting into a sweet, warm piece of heaven fresh from the oven. The brownie and bar creations offered here are guaranteed to win you accolades at Christmastime and all year long.

BLACK & WHITE CHEESECAKE BARS

Black & White Cheesecake Bars

❄ **Bertille Cooper, California, Maryland**

Whenever it's my turn to make dessert for a holiday celebration, I get requests for these scrumptious bars. Everyone loves the combination of chocolate and cream cheese.

    2   cups (12 ounces) semisweet chocolate chips
  1/2   cup butter
    2   cups graham cracker crumbs
    1   package (8 ounces) cream cheese, softened
    1   can (14 ounces) sweetened condensed milk
    1   egg
    1   teaspoon vanilla extract

In a double boiler or microwave, melt chocolate chips and butter, stirring occasionally. Stir in the graham cracker crumbs. Set aside 1/4 cup for topping. Press the remaining crumbs into an ungreased 13-in. x 9-in. x 2-in. baking pan.

In a bowl, beat cream cheese until smooth. Gradually beat in milk, egg and vanilla. Pour over crust. Sprinkle with reserved crumbs. Bake at 325° for 25-30 minutes or until lightly browned. Cool. Refrigerate 3 hours or until completely chilled. Cut into bars. Store in the refrigerator.
Yield: 4 dozen.

Cappuccino Truffle Brownies

❄ **Karen Yetter, Oceanside, California**

I created these brownies by combining chocolate with my favorite beverage for a cooking contest. I was so pleased with the results, I knew the recipe was a keeper.

    2   squares (1 ounce *each*) semisweet chocolate
  1/2   cup butter, cubed

    2   eggs
  3/4   cup packed brown sugar
    1   teaspoon vanilla extract
  3/4   cup all-purpose flour
  1/2   teaspoon baking powder
  1/2   teaspoon ground cinnamon

FILLING:
    1   package (8 ounces) cream cheese, softened
  1/4   cup confectioners' sugar
    1   teaspoon instant coffee granules
    1   tablespoon hot water
    1   cup (6 ounces) semisweet chocolate chips
  1/2   teaspoon butter

GLAZE:
  1/2   cup semisweet chocolate chips
    1   teaspoon shortening
Whole blanched almonds

In a microwave, melt chocolate and butter; stir until smooth. Cool slightly. In a small bowl, beat the eggs, brown sugar and vanilla. Beat in chocolate mixture. Combine the flour, baking powder and cinnamon; stir into chocolate mixture.

Spread into a greased 9-in. square baking pan. Bake at 350° for 20-22 minutes or until a toothpick comes out clean. Cool on a wire rack.

For filling, in a large bowl, beat the cream cheese and confectioners' sugar until light and fluffy. Dissolve coffee in water. Stir into cream cheese mixture. In a microwave, melt chips and butter; stir until smooth. Beat into cream cheese mixture until smooth. Spread over brownies.

For glaze, in a microwave, melt chips and shortening; stir until smooth. Dip each almond halfway into glaze and place on a waxed paper-lined baking sheet. Let stand until chocolate is set. Drizzle remaining glaze over bars. Place almond in the center of each bar. Refrigerate leftovers.
Yield: 16 bars.

CAPPUCCINO TRUFFLE BROWNIES

CRANBERRY BOG BARS

Cranberry Bog Bars

❄ **Sally Wakefield, Bruceton Mills, West Virginia**

Sweet and chewy, these fun bars combine the flavors of oats, cranberries, brown sugar and pecans. I like to sprinkle the squares with confectioners' sugar before serving.

1-1/4	cups butter, softened, *divided*
1-1/2	cups packed brown sugar, *divided*
3-1/2	cups old-fashioned oats, *divided*
1	cup all-purpose flour
1	can (16 ounces) whole-berry cranberry sauce
1/2	cup finely chopped pecans

In a large bowl, cream 1 cup butter and 1 cup brown sugar until light and fluffy. Combine 2-1/2 cups oats and flour. Gradually add to creamed mixture until crumbly. Press into a greased 13-in. x 9-in. x 2-in. baking pan. Spread with cranberry sauce.

In a microwave-safe bowl, melt remaining butter; stir in the pecans and remaining brown sugar and oats. Sprinkle over cranberry sauce. Bake at 375° for 25-30 minutes or until lightly browned. Cool on a wire rack. Cut into bars.
Yield: 3 dozen.

Candied Orange Date Bars

❄ **Eunice Stoen, Decorah, Iowa**

My good friend gave me the recipe for these yummy, rich date bars. Candied orange slices give them a tangy zest while chopped dates and walnuts add that extra-special touch.

1	package (7 ounces) orange candy slices
1/2	cup sugar
2	tablespoons plus 1-3/4 cups all-purpose flour, *divided*
1/2	cup water
1/2	pound chopped dates
1	cup butter, softened
1	cup packed brown sugar
2	eggs
1	teaspoon baking soda
1/2	teaspoon salt
1/2	cup chopped walnuts

Confectioners' sugar

Cut orange slices horizontally in half, then into 1/4-in. pieces; set aside. In a saucepan, combine the sugar and 2 tablespoons flour. Stir in water until smooth. Add dates. Bring to a boil; cook and stir for 2 minutes or until thickened. Remove from the heat; cool.

In a large bowl, cream butter and brown sugar. Add eggs, one at a time, beating well after each addition. Combine the baking soda, salt and remaining flour; add to creamed mixture. Stir in walnuts.

Spread half of the batter into a greased 13-in. x 9-in. x 2-in. baking pan. Spread date mixture over batter; sprinkle with reserved orange pieces. Spread remaining batter over the top. Bake at 350° for 30-35 minutes or until a toothpick inserted near the center comes out clean. Cool on a wire rack. Dust with confectioners' sugar.
Yield: about 3 dozen.

Editor's Note: To make cutting orange slices easier, use a kitchen shears dipped in hot water. Or, first toss the slices in 1-2 tablespoons of confectioners' sugar; use a mesh strainer or colander to shake off excess sugar, then cut.

CANDIED ORANGE DATE BARS

BUTTERSCOTCH BROWNIES

Butterscotch Brownies

❄ Lois Culberson, Pana, Illinois

A tasty, portable treat, these brownies get an unusually rich flavor from the combination of butterscotch chips and fluffy marshmallows.

3/4	cup butter
1	cup butterscotch chips
1-1/2	cups all-purpose flour
2/3	cup packed brown sugar
2	teaspoons baking powder
1/4	teaspoon salt
2	eggs
2	teaspoons vanilla extract
2	cups miniature marshmallows
2	cups semisweet chocolate chips
1/2	cup chopped walnuts

In a saucepan, melt butter and butterscotch chips; stir until smooth. Cool. In a large bowl, combine the flour, brown sugar, baking powder and salt. Add the eggs, vanilla and butterscotch mixture; mix well (batter will be thick). Fold in marshmallows, chocolate chips and walnuts.

Spread into a well-greased 15-in. x 10-in. x 1-in. baking pan. Bake at 350° for 20-25 minutes or until a toothpick inserted near the center comes out clean. Cool on a wire rack. Cut into bars.

Peanut Brittle Bars

❄ Kristin Gleason, St. John, Kansas

Pairing the old-fashioned flavor of peanut brittle with yummy chocolate chips turns these bars into a satisfying treat and sought-after holiday gift.

1-1/2	cups all-purpose flour
1/2	cup whole wheat flour
1	cup packed brown sugar
1	teaspoon baking soda
1/4	teaspoon salt
1	cup butter

TOPPING:

2	cups salted peanuts
1	cup milk chocolate chips
1	jar (12-1/4 ounces) caramel ice cream topping
3	tablespoons all-purpose flour

In a large bowl, combine flours, brown sugar, baking soda and salt. Cut in butter until mixture resembles coarse crumbs. Pat into a greased 15-in. x 10-in. x 1-in. baking pan. Bake at 350° for 10-12 minutes or until golden brown.

Sprinkle peanuts and chocolate chips over warm crust. Combine caramel topping and flour; drizzle over top. Bake 12-16 minutes longer or until golden brown and bubbly. Cool on a wire rack. Cut into squares.

Yield: about 4 dozen.

Malted Milk Ball Brownies

❄ Mitzi Sentiff, Annapolis, Maryland

You don't have to be a kid to love these delicious brownies! Malted milk balls blended into the batter and sprinkled on top make them extra-special. These brownies are a great treat to bring to holiday parties at school.

1	package fudge brownie mix (13-inch x 9-inch pan size)
1-1/3	cups chopped malted milk balls, *divided*
1	cup (6 ounces) semisweet chocolate chips
2	tablespoons butter
2	tablespoons milk
1/4	teaspoon vanilla extract

Prepare brownie batter according to package directions; stir in 1 cup malted milk balls. Spread into a greased 13-in. x 9-in. x 2-in. baking pan.

Bake at 350° for 28-30 minutes or until a toothpick inserted 2 in. from an edge comes out with moist crumbs. Cool completely on a wire rack.

In a small saucepan, melt chocolate chips and butter over low heat. Remove from the heat. Stir in the milk and the vanilla. Spread over brownies. Sprinkle with the remaining malted milk balls. Refrigerate for 10-15 minutes or until set. Cut into bars.

Yield: 2 dozen.

CARAMEL CHIP BARS

Dark Chocolate Butterscotch Brownies

❄ **Kit Concilus, Meadville, Pennsylvania**

My daughters and I love homemade brownies. We experimented with many recipes and finally came up with this family favorite. The thick, satiny frosting and butterscotch chips are simply irresistible.

4	squares (1 ounce *each*) unsweetened chocolate
3/4	cup butter, cubed
2	cups sugar
3	egg whites
1-1/2	teaspoons vanilla extract
1	cup all-purpose flour
1	cup 60% cocoa bittersweet chocolate baking chips
1	cup butterscotch chips

GLAZE:

1	cup 60% cocoa bittersweet chocolate baking chips
1/4	cup butter, cubed

In a microwave-safe bowl, melt unsweetened chocolate and butter; stir until smooth. Cool slightly. In a large bowl, combine sugar and chocolate mixture. Stir in egg whites and vanilla. Stir in flour. Stir in chips.

Spread into a greased 13-in. x 9-in. x 2-in. baking pan. Bake at 350° for 25-30 minutes or until a toothpick inserted near the center comes out clean. Cool on a wire rack.

For glaze, melt baking chips and butter; stir until smooth. Immediately spread over brownies. Cool before cutting.

Yield: about 5 dozen.

Caramel Chip Bars

❄ **LaDonna Reed, Ponca City, Oklahoma**

It's fun to take a basic yellow cake mix and create something this scrumptious. Our whole family likes to eat these bars when they are cold, right out of the refrigerator. Pour a tall glass of milk to complement the yummy flavor.

1/2	cup butter
32	caramels
1	can (14 ounces) sweetened condensed milk
1	package (18-1/4 ounces) yellow cake mix
1/2	cup vegetable oil
2	eggs
2	cups miniature semisweet chocolate chips
1	cup vanilla *or* white chips
1	Heath candy bar (1.4 ounces), chopped

In a large saucepan, combine the butter, caramels and milk; cook and stir over medium-low heat until smooth. Cool.

In a large bowl, beat the cake mix, oil and eggs until blended. Stir in chips and chopped candy bar (dough will be stiff).

Press three-fourths into a greased 13-in. x 9-in. x 2-in. baking pan. Bake at 350° for 15 minutes. Place on a wire rack for 10 minutes.

Pour the caramel mixture over the crust. Drop remaining dough by spoonfuls onto the caramel layer. Bake brownies for 25-30 minutes or until edges are golden brown. Cool for 10 minutes; run a knife around the edges of the pan. Cool 40 minutes longer; cover and refrigerate for at least 1 hour or until serving.

Yield: 2 dozen.

DARK CHOCOLATE BUTTERSCOTCH BROWNIES

CARAMEL BUTTER-PECAN BARS

Caramel Butter-Pecan Bars

❄ **Mary Jean Hlavac, McFarland, Wisconsin**

These melt-in-your-mouth bars are simply to die for. They go together in a jiffy, and even though the chocolate layer takes time to harden (think make-ahead convenience), these treats are definitely worth the wait.

    2   cups all-purpose flour
    1   cup packed brown sugar
  3/4   cup cold butter
1-1/2   cups chopped pecans
    1   jar (12 ounces) caramel ice cream topping, warmed
    1   package (11-1/2 ounces) milk chocolate chips

In a bowl, combine flour and brown sugar; cut in butter until crumbly. Press into an ungreased 13-in. x 9-in. x 2-in. baking dish. Top with pecans. Drizzle caramel topping evenly over pecans.

Bake at 350° for 15-20 minutes or until caramel is bubbly. Place on a wire rack. Sprinkle with chocolate chips. Let stand for 5 minutes. Carefully spread chips over caramel layer. Cool at room temperature for at least 6 hours or until chocolate is set. Cut into bars.
Yield: 4 dozen.

Chop to it!

Chopping an ingredient before or after measuring it can make a difference in the outcome of the recipe. An easy way to remember is if the word "chopped" comes before the ingredient when listed in a recipe, chop the ingredient before measuring. If the word "chopped" comes after the ingredient, chop after measuring.

Holiday Cheesecake Bars

❄ **Kathy Dorman, Snover, Michigan**

Christmas officially arrives at our house when I make these melt-in-your-mouth bars. Red and green maraschino cherries add a jolly finish to each light and creamy morsel.

    2   cups all-purpose flour
  2/3   cup packed brown sugar
  2/3   cup cold butter
    1   cup chopped walnuts
FILLING:
    2   packages (8 ounces *each*) cream cheese, softened
  1/2   cup sugar
    2   eggs
  1/4   cup milk
    2   tablespoons lemon juice
    1   teaspoon vanilla extract
Sliced red and green maraschino cherries, optional

In a bowl, combine the flour and brown sugar; cut in butter until mixture resembles coarse crumbs. Stir in the walnuts. Reserve 1 cup. Press remaining crumbs onto the bottom of an ungreased 13-in. x 9-in. x 2-in. baking pan. Bake at 350° for 12 minutes.

Meanwhile, in a bowl, beat cream cheese and sugar until light and fluffy. Add eggs, one at a time, beating well after each addition. Beat in milk, lemon juice and vanilla; pour over crust. Sprinkle with reserved crumbs.

Bake 25-30 minutes longer or until edges are lightly browned and filling is almost set. Cool in pan on a wire rack. Cut into squares. Garnish with cherries if desired. Store in the refrigerator.
Yield: 2 dozen.

HOLIDAY CHEESECAKE BARS

COBBLESTONE BROWNIES

Cobblestone Brownies

❄ **Phyllis Perry, Vassar, Kansas**

My family enjoys the combination of chocolate and coconut. So I stirred coconut extract into the brownie batter and added flaked coconut to the cream cheese filling. These fudgy bars are the tasty result!

       1   package fudge brownie mix (13-inch x 9-inch
           pan size)
    1/2   cup vegetable oil
       2   eggs
    1/2   teaspoon coconut extract
FILLING:
       1   package (8 ounces) cream cheese, softened
       2   eggs
       1   teaspoon coconut extract
       1   teaspoon vanilla extract
 3-3/4   cups confectioners' sugar
       1   cup flaked coconut

In a large bowl, beat the brownie mix, oil, eggs and extract on medium speed until blended (batter will be stiff). Set aside 1 cup for topping. Spread the remaining batter into a greased 13-in. x 9-in. x 2-in. baking pan. Bake at 350° for 10-15 minutes or until edges crack.

For filling, in a small bowl, beat the cream cheese, eggs, extracts and confectioners' sugar until smooth and creamy. Fold in the coconut. Carefully spread over brownies.

Drop reserved batter by teaspoonfuls over filling. Bake for 45-50 minutes or until a knife inserted near the center comes out clean. Cool on a wire rack. Store in the refrigerator.

Yield: 3 dozen.

Lemon-Lime Bars

❄ **Holly Wilkins, Lake Elmore, Vermont**

The refreshing taste of lemon and lime in these bars will remind you of a warm summer day during the cold winter season.

       1   cup butter, softened
    1/2   cup confectioners' sugar
       2   teaspoons grated lime peel
 1-3/4   cups all-purpose flour
    1/4   teaspoon salt
FILLING:
       4   eggs
 1-1/2   cups sugar
    1/4   cup all-purpose flour
    1/2   teaspoon baking powder
    1/3   cup lemon juice
       2   teaspoons grated lemon peel
Confectioners' sugar

In a bowl, cream butter and confectioners' sugar. Add lime peel; mix well. Combine flour and salt; gradually add to creamed mixture. Press into a greased 13-in. x 9-in. x 2-in. baking pan. Bake at 350° for 13-15 minutes or just until edges are lightly browned.

Meanwhile, in a bowl, beat eggs and sugar. Combine the flour and baking powder. Add to egg mixture with lemon juice and peel; beat until frothy. Pour over hot crust.

Bake for 20-25 minutes or until light golden brown. Cool on a wire rack. Dust with confectioners' sugar. Cut into squares. Store in the refrigerator.

Yield: 4 dozen.

LEMON-LIME BARS

COFFEE & CREAM BROWNIES

Coffee & Cream Brownies

❄️ Michelle Tiemstra, Lacombe, Alberta

A friend gave me the recipe for these tasty cake-like brownies topped with a creamy, coffee-enhanced filling and a chocolate glaze. I like to garnish each square with a coffee bean.

        1/2 cup butter, cubed
          3 squares (1 ounce *each*) unsweetened chocolate, chopped
          2 eggs
          1 cup sugar
          1 teaspoon vanilla extract
        2/3 cup all-purpose flour
        1/4 teaspoon baking soda
FILLING:
          1 tablespoon heavy whipping cream
          1 teaspoon instant coffee granules
          2 tablespoons butter, softened
          1 cup confectioners' sugar
GLAZE:
          1 cup (6 ounces) semisweet chocolate chips
        1/3 cup heavy whipping cream

In a saucepan over low heat, melt butter and chocolate; cool slightly. In a small bowl, beat eggs, sugar and vanilla; stir in the chocolate mixture. Combine flour and baking soda; add to the chocolate mixture. Spread into a greased 8-in. square baking pan. Bake at 350° for 25-30 minutes or until a toothpick inserted near the center comes out clean (do not overbake). Cool on a wire rack.

For filling, combine cream and coffee granules in a small bowl; stir until coffee is dissolved. In a small bowl, beat butter and confectioners' sugar. Add coffee mixture; beat until creamy. Spread over brownies.

In a small saucepan, combine chips and cream. Cook and stir over low heat until chocolate is melted and mixture is thickened. Cool slightly. Carefully spread over filling. Let stand for 30 minutes or until glaze is set. Cut into squares. Store in the refrigerator.

Yield: 16 servings.

Chewy Chip Bars

❄️ Eileen Sears, Eagle, Wisconsin

These sweet granola bars are chock-full of butterscotch and chocolate chips. The bars freeze well, so they make a quick snack or dessert that's easily portable and handy.

      4-1/2 cups old-fashioned oats
          1 cup all-purpose flour
        2/3 cup butter, softened
        1/2 cup honey
        1/3 cup packed brown sugar
          1 teaspoon baking soda
          1 teaspoon vanilla extract
          1 cup (6 ounces) semisweet chocolate chips
          1 cup butterscotch chips

In a large bowl, combine the first seven ingredients. Stir in the chips.

Press into a greased 13-in. x 9-in. x 2-in. baking pan. Bake at 325° for 18-22 minutes or until golden brown. Cool on a wire rack for 10 minutes; cut into bars. Cool completely in the pan.

Yield: 3 dozen.

Apple Walnut Squares

❄️ Jennifer Dzubinski, San Antonio, Texas

If you need a homespun snack or bake sale treat that can be assembled in a hurry, try these moist, nutty bars. The squares are sweet, flavorful and loaded with chopped apple and nuts.

        1/2 cup butter, softened
          1 cup sugar
          1 egg
          1 cup all-purpose flour
        1/2 teaspoon baking powder
        1/2 teaspoon baking soda
        1/2 teaspoon ground cinnamon
          1 medium tart apple, peeled and chopped
        3/4 cup chopped walnuts

APPLE WALNUT SQUARES

In a large bowl, cream butter and sugar until creamy. Beat in egg. Combine flour, baking powder, baking soda and cinnamon; gradually add to the creamed mixture, just until combined. Stir in apple and walnuts.

Pour into a greased 8-in. square baking dish. Bake at 350° for 35-40 minutes or until a toothpick inserted near the center comes out clean. Cool on a wire rack.

Yield: 16 servings.

Chocolate Chip Marshmallow Bars

❄️ **Sara Yoder, Apple Creek, Ohio**

With marshmallows and chocolate chips, these melt-in-your-mouth bars appeal to kids of all ages. They disappear fast wherever I take them.

1	cup shortening
3/4	cup sugar
3/4	cup packed brown sugar
2	eggs
1	teaspoon vanilla extract
2-1/4	cups all-purpose flour
1	teaspoon baking soda
1	teaspoon salt
2	cups miniature marshmallows
1-1/2	cups semisweet chocolate chips
3/4	cup chopped walnuts

In a large bowl, cream shortening and sugars until light and fluffy. Add eggs, one at a time, beating well after each addition. Beat in vanilla. Combine the flour, baking soda and salt; gradually add to creamed mixture and mix well. Stir in the marshmallows, chips and walnuts.

Spread into a greased 13-in. x 9-in. x 2-in. baking pan. Bake at 350° for 25-30 minutes or until golden brown. Cool on a wire rack. Cut into bars.

Yield: 3 dozen.

Caramel Fudge Brownies

❄️ **Priscilla Renfrow, Wilson, North Carolina**

These brownies are so rich and yummy, you'll never guess they're actually lighter than most. The caramel is a nice surprise most folks enjoy.

4	squares (1 ounce *each*) unsweetened chocolate
3	egg whites, lightly beaten
1	cup sugar
2	jars (2-1/2 ounces *each*) prune baby food
1	teaspoon vanilla extract
1/2	teaspoon salt
1/2	cup all-purpose flour
1/4	cup chopped walnuts
6	tablespoons fat-free caramel ice cream topping
9	tablespoons reduced-fat whipped topping

In a microwave or saucepan, melt chocolate; stir until smooth. In a bowl, combine the egg whites, sugar, melted chocolate, prunes, vanilla and salt; mix well. Stir in flour until just moistened.

Pour into an 8-in. square baking pan coated with cooking spray. Sprinkle with walnuts. Bake at 350° for 30-32 minutes or until the top springs back when lightly touched. Cool on a wire rack. Cut into squares; drizzle with caramel topping and dollop with whipped topping.

Yield: 9 servings.

CARAMEL FUDGE BROWNIES

CREAM CHEESE BROWNIES

For frosting, in a microwave-safe bowl, melt the butter and chocolate. Cool slightly; stir in confectioners' sugar and enough milk to achieve spreading consistency. Frost brownies. **Yield:** 16 brownies.

Cream Cheese Brownies

❄ **Carol Gillespie, Chambersburg, Pennsylvania**

These soft, cream cheese brownies are sure to delight. You'll never want to try another brownie recipe after eating these delicious treats.

      1   package fudge brownie mix (13-inch x 9-inch pan size)
  1/2   cup vanilla *or* white chips
FILLING:
      1   package (3 ounces) cream cheese, softened
      2   tablespoons butter, softened
  1/4   cup sugar
      1   egg
      1   tablespoon all-purpose flour
  1/2   teaspoon orange extract
FROSTING:
      2   tablespoons butter
      1   ounce unsweetened chocolate
      1   ounce semisweet chocolate
      1   cup confectioners' sugar
      2   to 3 tablespoons milk

Prepare brownies according to package directions for cake-like brownies; fold in chips. Spread half of the batter into a greased 13-in. x 9-in. x 2-in. baking pan.

In a small bowl, beat the cream cheese, butter and sugar until smooth. Beat in egg, flour and orange extract.

Carefully spread cream cheese mixture over batter. Drop remaining brownie batter by tablespoonfuls over cream cheese layer. Cut through batter with a knife to swirl.

Bake at 350° for 30-35 minutes or until a toothpick inserted near the center comes out almost clean. Cool on a wire rack.

Caramel-Cashew Cake Bars

❄ **Marlene Collins, Detroit Lakes, Minnesota**

These rich bars are a hit with everyone who tries them. The moist, cake-like crust pairs well with the chewy caramel and salty cashews.

  3/4   cup all-purpose flour
  1/2   cup sugar
  1/2   cup packed brown sugar
  1/2   teaspoon baking powder
  1/4   teaspoon salt
      2   eggs
  1/2   cup salted cashews, chopped
CASHEW TOPPING:
  1/2   cup salted cashews, chopped
  1/4   cup packed brown sugar
      2   tablespoons butter, melted
4-1/2   teaspoons heavy whipping cream

In a large bowl, combine the flour, sugars, baking powder and salt. Beat in the eggs just until combined. Fold in the cashews. Spread into a greased 8-in. square baking dish.

Bake at 350° for 20-25 minutes or until top springs back when lightly touched.

In a small bowl, combine the topping ingredients. Spread over cake. Broil for 1-2 minutes or until bubbly and lightly browned. Cut into bars while warm. Cool on a wire rack.

Yield: 16 bars.

CARAMEL-CASHEW CAKE BARS

MINT-FILLED BROWNIES

Chocolate Sauce Brownies

❄️ **Vickie Overby, Wahpeton, North Dakota**

These tender brownies are loaded with crunchy nuts and topped with sweet frosting.

      1/2   cup butter, softened
         1   cup sugar
         4   eggs
         1   can (16 ounces) chocolate syrup
         1   teaspoon vanilla extract
         1   cup plus 1 tablespoon all-purpose flour
      1/2   teaspoon baking powder
         1   cup chopped pecans *or* walnuts
FROSTING:
         1   cup sugar
         6   tablespoons milk
         6   tablespoons butter
      1/2   cup semisweet chocolate chips

In a bowl, cream butter and sugar. Add eggs, one at a time, beating well after each addition. Stir in chocolate syrup and vanilla. Combine flour and baking powder; add to the creamed mixture and mix well. Stir in nuts.

Pour into a greased 15-in. x 10-in. x 1-in. baking pan. Bake at 350° for 20-25 minutes or until a toothpick inserted near the center comes out clean. Cool on a wire rack.

For frosting, combine the sugar, milk and butter in a heavy saucepan. Bring to a boil over medium heat; boil for 1 minute. Remove from the heat. Add chocolate chips; stir or whisk for 5 minutes or until smooth. Spread over brownies.

Yield: 5 dozen.

Mint-Filled Brownies

❄️ **Edith Holmes, Brookfield, Massachusetts**

This refreshing treat has a creamy peppermint filling, making it the perfect dessert to serve following a traditional holiday meal. Use food coloring to tint the filling green for a festive look.

      1/3   cup shortening
         1   cup sugar
      1/2   teaspoon vanilla extract
         2   eggs
         2   squares (1 ounce *each*) unsweetened chocolate, melted and cooled
         1   tablespoon half-and-half cream
      2/3   cup all-purpose flour
      1/4   teaspoon salt
      1/3   cup chopped walnuts
      1/4   cup chopped raisins
FILLING:
   1-1/2   cups confectioners' sugar
         2   tablespoons hot milk
         1   teaspoon butter, melted
      1/2   to 3/4 teaspoon peppermint extract
Green food coloring, optional

In a bowl, cream the shortening, sugar and vanilla. Add the eggs; mix well. Beat in the chocolate and cream. Combine the flour and salt; add to creamed mixture. Stir in walnuts and raisins.

Spread into two greased and floured 9-in. square baking pans. Bake at 350° for 15-20 minutes or until a toothpick inserted near the center comes out clean. Cool for 10 minutes before removing from pans to wire racks to cool completely.

Combine the filling ingredients; spread over one brownie layer. Top with second layer. Chill before cutting.

Yield: 2 dozen.

CHOCOLATE SAUCE BROWNIES

APPLE PIE BARS

In a large bowl, toss the apples, sugar, flour, cinnamon and nutmeg; spread over the crust. Roll out remaining pastry to fit top of pan; place over filling. Trim edges; brush edges between pastry with water or milk; pinch to seal. Cut slits in top.

Bake at 375° for 45-50 minutes or until golden brown. Cool on a wire rack. Combine glaze ingredients until smooth; drizzle over bars before cutting.

Yield: about 2 dozen.

Chocolate-Drizzled Cherry Bars

❄ **Janice Heikkila, Deer Creek, Minnesota**

I've been making bars since I was in third grade, but these are special. I bake them for my church's Christmas party every year. Folks always rave about them and ask for a copy of the recipe.

      2 cups all-purpose flour
      2 cups quick-cooking oats
  1-1/2 cups sugar
  1-1/4 cups butter, softened
      1 can (21 ounces) cherry pie filling
      1 teaspoon almond extract
    1/4 cup semisweet chocolate chips
    3/4 teaspoon shortening

In a bowl, combine flour, oats, sugar and butter until crumbly. Set aside 1-1/2 cups for topping. Press remaining crumb mixture into an ungreased 13-in. x 9-in. x 2-in. baking dish. Bake at 350° for 15-18 minutes or until edges begin to brown.

Apple Pie Bars

❄ **Janet English, Pittsburgh, Pennsylvania**

This is one of many wonderful recipes my mother handed down to me. These delicious bars, with their flaky crust and scrumptious fruit filling, are the perfect way to serve apple pie to a crowd.

      4 cups all-purpose flour
      1 teaspoon salt
      1 teaspoon baking powder
      1 cup shortening
      4 egg yolks
      2 tablespoons lemon juice
      8 to 10 tablespoons cold water
FILLING:
      7 cups finely chopped peeled apples
      2 cups sugar
    1/4 cup all-purpose flour
      2 teaspoons ground cinnamon
Dash ground nutmeg
GLAZE:
      1 cup confectioners' sugar
      1 tablespoon milk
      1 tablespoon lemon juice

In a large bowl, combine flour, salt and baking powder. Cut in shortening until mixture resembles coarse crumbs. In a small bowl, whisk egg yolks, lemon juice and water; gradually add to flour mixture, tossing with a fork until dough forms a ball. Divide in half. Chill for 30 minutes.

Roll out one portion of dough between two large sheets of waxed paper into a 17-in. x 12-in. rectangle. Transfer to an ungreased 15-in. x 10-in. x 1-in. baking pan. Press pastry onto the bottom and up the sides of pan; trim pastry even with top edge.

CHOCOLATE-DRIZZLED CHERRY BARS

CEREAL COOKIE BARS

Stir in chocolate chips, raisins and baking bits. Press into two greased 15-in. x 10-in. x 1-in. pans. Cool for 30 minutes before cutting.
Yield: 6 dozen.

Polka-Dot Cookie Bars

❄ **Elizabeth Poire, Kailua-Kona, Hawaii**

When you're serving a group, these lightly sweet bars are a lot easier to make than fussing with individual cookies. To please true chocolate lovers, substitute semisweet chips for the vanilla chips.

    1   cup butter, softened
  3/4   cup sugar
  3/4   cup packed brown sugar
    2   eggs
  1/2   teaspoon almond extract
2-1/4   cups all-purpose flour
  1/3   cup baking cocoa
    1   teaspoon baking soda
  1/2   teaspoon salt
    1   package (10 to 12 ounces) vanilla *or* white chips

In a large bowl, cream butter and sugars until light and fluffy. Add eggs, one at a time, beating well after each addition. Beat in extract. Combine the flour, cocoa, baking soda and salt; gradually add to the creamed mixture. Set aside 1/4 cup vanilla chips; stir remaining chips into batter.

Spread in a greased 15-in. x 10-in. x 1-in. baking pan. Sprinkle with reserved chips. Bake at 375° for 18-23 minutes or until a toothpick inserted near the center comes out clean. Cool on a wire rack. Cut into bars.
Yield: 4 dozen.

In a bowl, combine pie filling and extract; carefully spread over crust. Sprinkle with reserved crumb mixture.

Bake 20-25 minutes longer or until edges and topping are lightly browned. In a microwave or heavy saucepan, melt chocolate chips and shortening; stir until smooth. Drizzle over warm bars. Cool completely on a wire rack.
Yield: 3 dozen.

Cereal Cookie Bars

❄ **Connie Craig, Lakewood, Washington**

These chewy crowd-pleasers feature all sorts of goodies, including chocolate chips, raisins, coconut and candy-coated baking bits. For a more colorful look, press the baking bits on top of the bars instead of stirring them into the cereal mixture.

    9   cups crisp rice cereal
6-1/2   cups quick-cooking oats
    1   cup cornflakes
    1   cup flaked coconut
    2   packages (one 16 ounces, one 10-1/2 ounces) miniature marshmallows
    1   cup butter, cubed
  1/2   cup honey
  1/2   cup chocolate chips
  1/2   cup raisins
  1/2   cup M&M's miniature baking bits

In a large bowl, combine the cereal, oats, cornflakes and coconut; set aside.

In a large saucepan, cook and stir the marshmallows and butter over low heat until melted and smooth. Stir in honey. Pour over cereal mixture; stir until coated. Cool for 5 minutes.

POLKA-DOT COOKIE BARS

PEANUT BUTTER CEREAL BARS

Peanut Butter Cereal Bars

❄ **Denise Moore, Nepean, Ontario**

I received this recipe from my mother, and it's now part of my annual Christmas baking routine. For a little variety, form the mixture into balls with chocolate caps. One batch is never enough!

```
1/4    cup packed brown sugar
1/4    cup creamy peanut butter
1/4    cup light corn syrup
2-1/2  teaspoons butter, divided
  1    cup crisp rice cereal
1/4    cup chopped pecans
1/2    cup semisweet chocolate chips
```

In a small saucepan, combine the brown sugar, peanut butter, corn syrup and 1-1/2 teaspoons butter. Bring to a boil over medium heat, stirring constantly. Remove from the heat; stir in the cereal and pecans. Press into a 9-in. x 5-in. x 3-in. loaf pan coated with cooking spray.

In a microwave or saucepan, melt the chocolate chips and remaining butter; stir until smooth. Spread over cereal mixture; cool. Cut into bars. Store in the refrigerator.

Yield: 8 bars.

Pumpkin Cheesecake Bars

❄ **Agnes Jasa, Malabar, Florida**

This recipe caught my eye and was extremely popular at the annual Christmas party I attend. It's a great dessert for this time of year.

```
  1    cup all-purpose flour
1/3    cup packed brown sugar
  5    tablespoons cold butter
  1    cup finely chopped pecans
  1    package (8 ounces) cream cheese, softened
3/4    cup sugar
1/2    cup canned pumpkin
  2    eggs
  1    teaspoon vanilla extract
1-1/2  teaspoons ground cinnamon
  1    teaspoon ground allspice
```

In a large bowl, combine flour and brown sugar. Cut in butter until crumbly. Stir in pecans; set aside 3/4 cup for topping.

Press remaining crumb mixture into a greased 8-in. square baking pan. Bake at 350° for 15 minutes or until edges are lightly browned. Cool on a wire rack.

In a large bowl, beat cream cheese and sugar until smooth. Beat in the pumpkin, eggs, vanilla, cinnamon and allspice. Pour over crust. Sprinkle with reserved crumb mixture.

Bake for 30-35 minutes or until golden brown. Cool on a wire rack. Cut into bars. Store in the refrigerator.

Yield: 16 bars.

Cashew Blondies

❄ **Kathey Skarie, Vergas, Minnesota**

These easy-to-make white chocolate brownies are a hit at potlucks and other gatherings—I always come home with an empty plate and lots of compliments.

```
  2    eggs
2/3    cup sugar
  1    teaspoon vanilla extract
  8    squares (1 ounce each) white baking chocolate,
       melted and cooled
1/3    cup butter, melted
1-1/2  cups all-purpose flour
1-1/2  teaspoons baking powder
1/4    teaspoon salt
1/2    to 1 cup chopped salted cashews or pecans
```

In a large bowl, beat the eggs, sugar and vanilla on medium speed for 1 minute. Beat in chocolate and butter. Combine the flour, baking powder and salt; gradually add to chocolate mixture. Stir in cashews.

Spread mixture into a greased 9-in. square baking pan. Bake at 350° for 25-30 minutes or until a toothpick inserted near the center comes out clean. Cool on a wire rack. Cut into bars.

Yield: 2 dozen.

CHRISTMAS SWEETS

7

You'll be crowned candy-maker of the year with these lip-smacking homemade confections. From simply sweet to absolutely divine, these tiny bites of bliss will tickle everybody's taste buds this season.

CREAM CHEESE CANDIES

Cream Cheese Candies

❄️ Katie Koziolek, Hartland, Minnesota

This four-ingredient recipe was recommended by friends and shared throughout our neighborhood. The rich, simple mints are often seen at wedding receptions and graduation parties, and they make a perfect, last-minute addition to holiday candy trays.

   1   package (3 ounces) cream cheese, softened
1/4   teaspoon peppermint *or* almond extract
   3   cups confectioners' sugar
Green and red colored sugar, optional

In a small bowl, combine cream cheese and extract. Beat in 1-1/2 cups confectioners' sugar. Knead in remaining confectioners' sugar until smooth. Shape into 1/2-in. balls. Roll in colored sugar if desired.

    Place on ungreased baking sheets and flatten with a fork. Let stand for 1 hour to harden. Store in an airtight container in the refrigerator.
    Yield: 6 dozen.

Gumdrop Fudge

❄️ Jennifer Short, Omaha, Nebraska

Making candy is one of my favorite things to do during the holidays. This sweet white fudge is as easy to put together as it is beautiful to serve.

1-1/2   pounds white candy coating
   1   can (14 ounces) sweetened condensed milk
1/8   teaspoon salt

1-1/2   teaspoons vanilla extract
1-1/2   cups chopped gumdrops

Line a 9-in. square pan with foil; set aside. In a saucepan, heat the candy coating, milk and salt over low heat until melted. Remove from the heat; stir in vanilla and gumdrops.
    Spread into prepared pan. Cover and refrigerate until firm. Using foil, remove fudge from the pan; cut into 1-in. squares. Store at room temperature.
    Yield: about 3 pounds.

Holiday Spruce Cookies

❄️ Jeanette Alessi, Orange, California

These easy treats won first prize at our last cookie exchange for "prettiest and best tasting" cookie! They're fun to make, and kids will have a blast trimming them with red-hot candy ornaments.

 36   large marshmallows
1/2   cup butter, cubed
  1   to 2 teaspoons green food coloring
  1   teaspoon almond extract
  4   cups cornflakes
Red-hot candies
 12   Tootsie Roll Midgees, cut in half, optional

In a heavy saucepan, combine the marshmallows, butter, food coloring and almond extract; cook and stir over low heat until smooth. Remove from the heat; gently stir in cornflakes until well coated. Drop by tablespoonfuls onto waxed paper.
    Using a 3-in. Christmas tree cookie cutter, shape into trees. Add red-hots for ornaments. Press a Tootsie Roll half into the base for tree trunk if desired.
    Yield: about 2 dozen.

HOLIDAY SPRUCE COOKIES

CHEWY ALMOND NOUGAT

medium heat, combine sugar and corn syrup. Cook and stir until sugar is dissolved and mixture comes to a boil, about 15 minutes. (If sugar crystals are present, cover and boil for 1-2 minutes to allow steam to wash crystals down.) With a clean spoon, cook and stir over medium-high heat until a candy thermometer reads 275° (soft-crack stage), about 15 minutes longer.

Pour over mixture in bowl (do not scrape saucepan). With a large wooden spoon, stir until blended. Combine butter and vanilla; gradually add to almond mixture until blended. Transfer to prepared pan. Let stand at room temperature for several hours or until firm. Cut into squares. Wrap in plastic wrap or waxed paper if desired.

Yield: about 5-1/2 pounds.

Chewy Almond Nougat

❄ **Vera Kramer, Jenera, Ohio**

I've been making this candy for years. It continues to be a tradition for when the kids and grandkids come home for the holidays. I substitute pistachios for the almonds with wonderful results.

```
  3     egg whites
1-1/2   cups sugar
1-1/4   cups light corn syrup
  1/4   cup water
ALMOND MIXTURE:
  3     cups sugar
  3     cups light corn syrup
  1/2   cup butter, melted
  4     teaspoons vanilla extract
  3     cups slivered almonds, toasted
  1     teaspoon salt
```

Heavily butter a 15-in. x 10-in. x 1-in. pan; set aside. Heavily butter a large bowl; set aside. In a stand mixer, beat egg whites until stiff peaks form. In a heavy saucepan over medium heat, combine the sugar, corn syrup and water. Cook and stir until sugar is dissolved and mixture comes to a boil, about 10 minutes. (If sugar crystals are present, cover and boil for 1-2 minutes to allow steam to wash crystals down.) Cook, without stirring, until a candy thermometer reads 238° (soft-ball stage), about 6-8 minutes.

With mixer running carefully and slowly add hot liquid in a steady stream over egg whites. Beat 10 minutes longer or until mixture holds its shape and is lukewarm. (Mixture will be beginning to lose its gloss.) Transfer to prepared bowl.

For almond mixture, in a large heavy saucepan over

Potato Chip Clusters

❄ **Donna Brockett, Kingfisher, Oklahoma**

Three offbeat ingredients add up to one unique, lip-smacking, no-bake treat. These super-easy, sweet-and-salty candy clusters make for merry munching during holiday trips or parties. They travel well in containers without melting or getting soft, making them an ideal hostess gift.

```
  9    squares (1 ounce each) white baking chocolate
  2    cups crushed potato chips
1/2    cup chopped pecans
```

In a large microwave-safe bowl, melt white chocolate. Stir in potato chips and pecans. Drop by tablespoonfuls onto waxed paper-lined baking sheets. Refrigerate until set.

Yield: about 3 dozen.

POTATO CHIP CLUSTERS

PEPPERMINT TAFFY

Peppermint Taffy

❄ **Elaine Chichura, Kingsley, Pennsylvania**

Get kids involved in an old-fashioned taffy pull with this fun recipe. The soft, chewy taffy has a minty flavor and won't stick to the wrapper. You can easily change the color and flavor, too.

2-1/2   cups sugar
1-1/2   cups light corn syrup
    4   teaspoons white vinegar
  1/4   teaspoon salt
  1/2   cup evaporated milk
  1/4   teaspoon peppermint oil
Red food coloring

Butter a 15-in. x 10-in. x 1-in. pan; set aside. In a heavy large saucepan, combine the sugar, corn syrup, vinegar and salt. Cook and stir over low heat until sugar is dissolved. Bring to a boil over medium heat. Slowly add the milk; cook and stir until a candy thermometer reads 248° (firm-ball stage).

Remove from the heat; stir in peppermint oil and food coloring, keeping face away from mixture, as odor is very strong. Pour into prepared pan. Let stand for 8 minutes or until cool enough to handle.

With well-buttered fingers, quickly pull candy until firm but pliable (color will become light pink). Pull into a 1/2-in. rope; cut into 1-in. pieces. Wrap each in waxed paper.

Yield: 1-3/4 pounds.

Cinnamon Almond Brittle

❄ **Lynette Kleinschmidt, Litchfield, Minnesota**

It simply wouldn't be Christmas at our house without this old-time favorite twist on peanut brittle. No one believes how easy it is to make...and it doesn't stick to your teeth!

    2   cups sugar
  3/4   cup light corn syrup
  1/4   cup water
    3   tablespoons butter, cubed
    2   teaspoons ground cinnamon
  1/2   teaspoon salt
    3   cups slivered almonds, toasted
1-1/2   teaspoons baking soda
    1   teaspoon vanilla extract

Butter two baking sheets and keep warm in a 200° oven. In a large saucepan, combine the sugar, corn syrup and water. Cook and stir over medium heat until a candy thermometer reads 240° (soft-ball stage). Stir in the butter, cinnamon, salt and almonds; cook and stir until mixture reaches 300° (hard-crack stage), brushing down sides of pan with water as needed.

Remove from the heat; stir in baking soda and vanilla. Quickly pour onto prepared baking sheets. Spread with a buttered metal spatula to 1/4-in. thickness. Cool; break into pieces. Store in an airtight container.

Yield: about 2 pounds.

Editor's Note: We recommend that you test your candy thermometer before each use by bringing water to a boil; the thermometer should read 212°. Adjust your recipe temperature up or down based on your test.

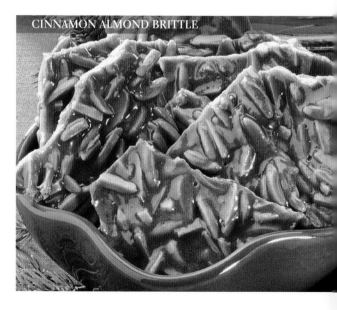
CINNAMON ALMOND BRITTLE

CRANBERRY NUT BARK

In a small bowl, beat cream cheese and pineapple until combined. Cover and refrigerate for 30 minutes.

Roll into 1-in. balls; roll in coconut. Refrigerate for 6 hours or overnight.

Yield: about 2 dozen.

Goody-Goody Gumdrops

❄ Sue Ann Bunt, Painted Post, New York

These homemade, jewel-toned squares are softer than store-bought gumdrops. But their fantastic flavor has true old-fashioned flair people love.

> 3 envelopes unflavored gelatin
> 1-1/4 cups water, *divided*
> 1-1/2 cups sugar
> 1/4 to 1/2 teaspoon peppermint extract
> Green and red food coloring
> Additional sugar

In a small bowl, sprinkle gelatin over 1/2 cup water; let stand for 5 minutes. In a saucepan, bring sugar and remaining water to a boil over medium heat, stirring constantly. Add the gelatin; reduce heat. Simmer and stir for 5 minutes. Remove from the heat and stir in extract.

Divide mixture into two bowls; add four drops green food coloring to one bowl and four drops red to the other. Pour into two greased 8-in. x 4-in. x 2-in. loaf pans. Chill 3 hours or until firm.

Loosen edges from pan with a knife; turn onto a sugared board. Cut into 1/2-in. cubes; roll in sugar. Let stand at room temperature, uncovered, for 3-4 hours, turning every hour so all sides dry. Cover and chill.

Yield: about 1 pound.

Cranberry Nut Bark

❄ Betty Richardson, Walnut Cove, North Carolina

Studded with chunks of cranberries and nuts, this sweet, creamy confection is the perfect last-minute gift! It's ready to wrap in less than 30 minutes, and everyone who tries it asks for more—and requests the recipe, too.

> 1 pound white candy coating, coarsely chopped
> 1 cup dried cranberries
> 1 cup coarsley chopped macadamia nuts *or* pistachios, toasted

In a large microwave-safe bowl, melt candy coating at 70% power for 1 minute; stir. Microwave at 30-second intervals, stirring until smooth. Stir in cranberries and nuts.

Spread mixture onto a waxed paper-lined baking sheet. Refrigerate for 20 minutes. Break into small pieces; store in airtight containers.

Yield: about 1-3/4 pounds.

Editor's Note: This recipe was tested in a 1,100-watt microwave.

Pineapple Coconut Snowballs

❄ Marlene Rhodes, Colorado Springs, Colorado

This three-ingredient treat is a cinch to whip up during the busy holiday season. Canned pineapple adds a refreshing taste to the frosty-looking finger food.

> 1 package (8 ounces) cream cheese, softened
> 1 can (8 ounces) crushed pineapple, well drained
> 2-1/2 cups flaked coconut

GOODY-GOODY GUMDROPS

MINTY SNOWMEN

colored dough to form hats, scarves and earmuffs as desired. Use colored sprinkles and cake decorator candies to make eyes, nose and buttons.

Yield: 8 snowmen.

Minty Meringue Drops

❄️ **Karen Wissing, Vashon, Washington**

These pretty mint green drops are dotted with mint chocolate chips. My kids don't consider it the Christmas season until I make them.

>   2   egg whites
>   1/4   teaspoon cream of tartar
>   3/4   cup sugar
>   1/8   teaspoon vanilla extract
>   2   to 6 drops green food coloring, optional
>   1   package (10 ounces) mint chocolate chips

Lightly grease baking sheets or line with parchment paper; set aside.

In a large bowl, beat egg whites until foamy. Add cream of tartar, beating until soft peaks form. Gradually beat in sugar, 1 tablespoon at a time, until stiff peaks form. Beat in vanilla and food coloring if desired. Fold in the chocolate chips.

Drop by rounded tablespoonfuls 2 in. apart onto prepared baking sheets. Bake at 250° for 30-35 minutes or until dry to the touch. Remove to wire racks to cool. Store in an airtight container.

Yield: about 2-1/2 dozen.

Editor's Note: If mint chocolate chips are not available, place 2 cups (12 ounces) semisweet chocolate chips and 1/4 teaspoon peppermint extract in a plastic bag; seal and toss to coat. Allow chips to stand for 24-48 hours.

Minty Snowmen

❄️ **Shelly Rynearson, Dousman, Wisconsin**

The theme of last year's holiday kickoff party was snowmen and snowflakes. These cute little snowman mints were fun to make and brought lots of smiles.

>   1   tablespoon butter, softened
>   1   tablespoon light corn syrup
>   1/2   teaspoon mint extract
>   1/8   teaspoon salt
>   1   cup confectioners' sugar
>   1   drop blue food coloring
>   1   drop yellow food coloring
>   1   drop red food coloring
> Colored sprinkles and cake decorator candies

In a small bowl, combine the butter, corn syrup, extract and salt. Gradually stir in confectioners' sugar. Knead by hand for 1-2 minutes or until mixture becomes pliable.

Add blue food coloring to 1 tablespoon of dough; knead until blended. Add yellow food coloring to another tablespoon of dough and knead. Add red food coloring to another tablespoon of dough and knead. Leave remaining dough white.

Roll white dough into a log; remove one-fourth of the log and set aside. For the snowmen's bodies, divide the remaining log into 8 pieces and roll into balls. For the snowmen's heads, divide the reserved dough into 8 pieces and roll into balls. Stack 1 smaller ball on top of each larger ball. Use the

MINTY MERINGUE DROPS

SUGARPLUMS

In a microwave-safe bowl, melt candy coating at 70% power for 45 seconds; stir. Microwave at additional 15-second intervals, stirring until smooth. Stir in spearmint candy.

Spread mixture onto a waxed paper-lined baking sheet. Chill for 8-10 minutes. Break into small pieces; store in airtight containers.

Yield: 1-1/4 pounds.

Crunchy Pecan Drops

❄ **Glenda Gibson, Columbia, Missouri**

My family looks forward to this candy I make every Christmas. For a chocolaty treat, I like to use chocolate kisses in place of the vanilla chips.

> 5 cups sugar
> 1 can (12 ounces) evaporated milk
> 1/2 cup butter, cubed
> 2 packages (10 to 12 ounces *each*) vanilla *or* white chips
> 1 jar (7 ounces) marshmallow creme
> 3 teaspoons vanilla extract
> 6 cups chopped pecans

In a large heavy saucepan, bring the sugar, milk and butter to a boil over medium-low heat, stirring constantly. Boil and stir for 8 minutes. Add the remaining ingredients; stir until combined. Cool for 10 minutes.

Quickly form by tablespoonfuls onto waxed paper-lined baking sheets. If mixture becomes too thick, reheat slightly. Refrigerate for 20 minutes or until firm. Store in an airtight container in the refrigerator.

Yield: about 14 dozen.

Sugarplums

❄ **Suzanne McKinley, Lyons, Georgia**

When our kids read about sugarplums in a holiday tale, they were intrigued...and so was I! In short order, I figured out a no-bake way to make the sweets from dried fruits and nuts.

> 1 package (15 ounces) raisins
> 1 package (12 ounces) pitted prunes
> 1 package (8 ounces) dried mixed fruit
> 1-1/2 cups chopped pecans
> Sugar

In a food processor, coarsely chop raisins, prunes, mixed fruit and pecans. Transfer to a bowl, mix well. Roll into 1-in. balls, then roll in sugar. Place on waxed paper and let stand at room temperature for 4 hours. Store in an airtight container. Roll in additional sugar before serving if desired.

Yield: about 8 dozen.

Spearmint Crunch

❄ **Rose Randall, Derry, Pennsylvania**

I love preparing food for the holidays, so I start planning early. This is one of my all-time favorite recipes, and it's so easy to make. Kids can have fun crushing the spearmint candies.

> 1 pound white candy coating, coarsely chopped
> 3/4 cup crushed spearmint candy (4 ounces)

CRUNCHY PECAN DROPS

BUTTER MINTS

Butter Mints

❄️ Bev Schloneger, Dalton, Ohio

These creamy mints are as smooth as silk and melt in your mouth. As a wife and mother of three youngsters, I treasure treats like these that come together quickly but taste terrific.

> 1/2 cup butter, softened
> 1 package (1 pound) confectioners' sugar
> 1 tablespoon half-and-half cream *or* milk
> 1 teaspoon vanilla extract
> 1/4 teaspoon peppermint extract
> Red and green paste *or* liquid food coloring, optional

In a bowl, cream the butter. Gradually add sugar, cream and extracts; beat on medium speed for 3-4 minutes. If desired, divide dough into portions and knead in food coloring.

Form into balls by teaspoonfuls; flatten into patties, or roll between two pieces of waxed paper to 1/8-in. thickness and cut into desired shapes. Cover and refrigerate for several hours or overnight. Store in the refrigerator.
Yield: about 8 dozen.

Sugary Orange Peel

❄️ Alice Schmidlin, Banks, Oregon

These sugar-coated citrus strips attract lots of compliments whenever I set them out at parties. They're sweet and refreshing to the palate.

> 4 medium navel oranges
> 2 to 3 cups sugar, *divided*
> 1 cup water
> 1/2 teaspoon salt

> 1/2 cup semisweet chocolate chips, optional
> 2 teaspoons shortening, optional

With a knife, score the peel from each orange into quarters. With fingers, remove peel and white pith attached. Place peel in a saucepan; cover with water. Bring to a boil. Boil, uncovered, for 30 minutes. Drain and repeat twice.

Meanwhile, in another saucepan, combine 1 cup of sugar, water and salt. Bring to a boil; boil and stir for 2 minutes or until the sugar is dissolved. Drain peel and add to syrup. Bring to a boil; reduce heat. Simmer, uncovered, for 50-60 minutes or until syrup is almost all absorbed, stirring occasionally. (Watch carefully to prevent scorching.) Drain any remaining syrup.

Cool orange peel in a single layer on a foil-lined baking sheet for 1 hour. Cut into 1/8-in. to 1/4-in. strips. Sprinkle remaining sugar on an ungreased 15-in. x 10-in. x 1-in. baking pan. Sprinkle strips over sugar; toss to coat. Let stand for 8 hours or overnight, tossing occasionally.

If desired, melt chocolate chips and shortening. Dip one end of each orange strip into chocolate; let stand on waxed paper until chocolate hardens. Store in an airtight container for up to 3 weeks.
Yield: 5 cups.

Brown Sugar Cashew Fudge

❄️ Jennifer Adams, Plymouth, Massachusetts

This creamy, light-colored fudge, loaded with crunchy cashews, is a yummy variation of traditional chocolate...and it disappears just as fast!

> 1-1/2 teaspoons plus 1/4 cup butter, softened, *divided*
> 1 cup packed brown sugar
> 1/2 cup evaporated milk
> 2 tablespoons light corn syrup
> 2-1/2 cups confectioners' sugar
> 2 cups coarsely chopped salted cashews

Line a 9-in. square pan with foil and grease the foil with 1-1/2 teaspoons butter; set aside.

In a heavy saucepan, combine the brown sugar, milk, corn syrup and remaining butter. Cook and stir over medium heat until sugar is dissolved. Bring mixture to a rapid boil, stirring constantly for 5 minutes.

Remove from the heat. Gradually add confectioners' sugar; mix well. Fold in cashews. Immediately spread into prepared pan. Cool. Using foil, lift fudge out of pan. Cut into 1-in. squares. Refrigerate in an airtight container.
Yield: 3 dozen.

CINNAMON HARD CANDY

White Christmas Fudge

❄️ **Paula Truska, Jewett, Texas**

This smooth, sweet fudge is loaded with nuts and chewy fruit and is just perfect for holiday gift-giving.

    1   teaspoon plus 1/4 cup butter, *divided*
2-1/2   cups confectioners' sugar
    2/3 cup milk
    12   squares (1 ounce *each*) white baking chocolate, chopped
    1/4 teaspoon almond extract
    3/4 cup sliced almonds, toasted
    1/4 cup chopped dried apricots
    1/4 cup dried cherries
    1/4 cup dried cranberries

Line a 9-in. square pan with foil and grease the foil with 1 teaspoon butter; set aside. In a heavy saucepan, combine the confectioners' sugar, milk and remaining butter. Cook and stir over medium heat until combined. Bring to a boil; boil for 5 minutes without stirring. Reduce heat to low; stir in white chocolate and almond extract. Cook and stir until chocolate is melted.

Remove from the heat. Fold in the almonds, apricots, cherries and cranberries. Immediately spread into prepared pan. Refrigerate for 2 hours or until set. Using foil, lift fudge out of pan. Discard foil; cut fudge into 1-in. squares. Store in the refrigerator.

Yield: about 2 pounds.

Cinnamon Hard Candy

❄️ **Mary Ellen Geigley, Willcox, Arizona**

My Amish aunt made dozens of these spicy red squares for holiday gatherings when I was a tot. I'd always look for them glowing among the candies she'd carry in! Nowadays, I stir up her recipe for my own family.

    2   cups sugar
    1   cup water
    1/2 cup light corn syrup
    1/4 to 1/2 teaspoon cinnamon oil
    1/2 teaspoon red food coloring

In a large heavy saucepan, combine sugar, water and corn syrup. Bring to a boil over medium heat, stirring occasionally. Cover and cook for 3 minutes. Uncover and cook over medium-high heat, without stirring, until a candy thermometer reads 310° (hard-crack stage). Remove from the heat; stir in oil and food coloring, keeping face away from the mixture as the odor will be very strong.

Immediately pour onto a greased baking sheet. Quickly spread into a 13-in. x 9-in. rectangle. Using a sharp knife, score into 1-in. squares. Re-cut rectangle along scored lines until candy is cut into squares. Let stand at room temperature until dry. Separate into squares, using a knife if necessary.

Yield: 1 pound.

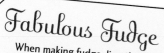

Fabulous Fudge
When making fudge, line the pan with foil so the fudge can easily be lifted out in one solid piece. Always cut fudge outside the pan to prevent knife scratches and to achieve evenly cut pieces.

WHITE CHRISTMAS FUDGE

ANISE HARD CANDY

Butterscotch Hard Candy

❄ **Darlene Smithers, Elkhart, Indiana**

I love making this classic butterscotch recipe. These irresistible bites are better than the store-bought variety...and they sure don't last long!

> 1 teaspoon plus 1 cup butter, *divided*
> 2-1/2 cups sugar
> 3/4 cup water
> 1/2 cup light corn syrup
> 1/4 cup honey
> 1/2 teaspoon salt
> 1/2 teaspoon rum extract

Butter a 15-in. x 10-in. x 1-in. baking pan with 1 teaspoon butter; set aside. Cube remaining butter and set aside.

In a heavy saucepan, combine the sugar, water and corn syrup. Cover and bring to a boil over medium heat without stirring. Cook, uncovered, until a candy thermometer reads 270° (soft-crack stage). Add the honey, salt and remaining butter; stir constantly until the mixture reaches 300° (hard-crack stage).

Remove from the heat. Stir in the rum extract. Pour into prepared pan without scraping; do not spread. Cool for 1-2 minutes or until the candy is almost set. Score into 1-in. squares; cool completely. Break squares apart. Store in an airtight container.

Yield: 1-1/2 pounds.

Editor's Note: We recommend that you test your candy thermometer before each use by bringing water to a boil; the thermometer should read 212°. Adjust your recipe temperature up or down based on your test.

Anise Hard Candy

❄ **Jobyna Carpenter, Poulso, Washington**

This old-fashioned hard candy became an annual Christmas project after I first prepared the recipe with a friend who made candy for a local shop. For a fun variation, substitute peppermint extract in place of the anise and green food coloring in place of the red.

> 1-1/2 teaspoons butter, softened
> 3/4 cup water
> 2/3 cup light corn syrup
> 2 cups sugar
> 1 teaspoon anise extract
> Red food coloring
> 2 to 3 tablespoons confectioners' sugar

Butter an 8-in. square baking pan with 1-1/2 teaspoons butter; set aside. In a large heavy saucepan, combine water, corn syrup and sugar. Bring to a boil over medium heat, stirring occasionally. Cover and cook for 3 minutes to dissolve any sugar crystals. Uncover; cook over medium-high heat, without stirring, until a candy thermometer reads 300° (hard-crack stage). Remove from the heat; stir in extract and food coloring (keep face away from mixture as odor is very strong).

Pour into prepared pan. Using a sharp knife, score into 3/4-in. squares. Cool. Separate into squares, using a sharp knife if necessary. Place confectioners' sugar in a baking pan; add candy and roll until coated. Brush off excess sugar with a pastry brush.

Store at room temperature in an airtight container.

Yield: about 1 pound (about 8 dozen).

Editor's Note: We recommend that you test your candy thermometer before each use by bringing water to a boil; the thermometer should read 212°. Adjust your recipe temperature up or down based on your test.

BUTTERSCOTCH HARD CANDY

NUTTY CARAMELS

Homemade Marshmallows

❄ Nancy Shields, Hillsdale, Michigan

My husband's grandmother fixed these fluffy marshmallows for special occasions. Since she had no electric mixer, beating the ingredients by hand for 30 minutes was truly a labor of love. Now, my husband makes them, and they're every bit as delicious!

> 2 cups cold water, *divided*
> 4 envelopes unflavored gelatin
> 4 cups sugar
> 1/8 teaspoon salt
> 2 teaspoons vanilla extract

Confectioners' sugar
Toasted flaked coconut *or* ground pecans, optional

In a large bowl, combine 3/4 cup of water and gelatin; set aside. In a large heavy saucepan over medium heat, combine sugar, salt and remaining water. Bring to a boil, stirring occasionally. Cover and continue cooking for 3 minutes to dissolve any sugar crystals. Uncover and cook on medium-high heat, without stirring, until a candy thermometer reads 270° (soft-crack stage). Remove from the heat and gradually add to gelatin. Beat on low speed for 3 minutes. Add vanilla; beat on medium for 10 minutes.

Spread mixture into a 13-in. x 9-in. x 2-in. pan sprinkled with confectioners' sugar. Cover and cool at room temperature for 6 hours or overnight. Cut into 1-in. squares; roll in coconut or nuts if desired. Store in airtight containers in a cool dry place.

Yield: about 8 dozen.

Nutty Caramels

❄ Lynn Nelson, Kasilof, Alaska

My cousin shared this quick and easy recipe with me. We make it every Christmas and include the caramels in gift baskets to share with family and friends.

> 1 teaspoon butter plus 1/4 cup butter, *divided*
> 1 cup sugar
> 1 cup light corn syrup
> 1 cup evaporated milk
> 1 cup chopped nuts
> 1 teaspoon vanilla extract

Melted milk chocolate

Line a 9-in. square pan with foil and grease the foil with 1 teaspoon butter; set aside. In a large heavy saucepan, combine the sugar, corn syrup, milk and remaining butter. Cook and stir over medium heat until sugar is dissolved. Bring to a rapid boil, stirring constantly, until a candy thermometer reads 248° (firm-ball stage).

Remove from the heat; stir in nuts and vanilla. Pour into prepared pan (do not scrape saucepan). Cool completely. Using foil, lift caramels out of pan; discard foil. Cut into small squares or diamonds. Drizzle each with chocolate if desired.

Yield: 1-1/2 pounds.

Editor's Note: We recommend that you test your candy thermometer before each use by bringing water to a boil; the thermometer should read 212°. Adjust your recipe temperature up or down based on your test.

HOMEMADE MARSHMALLOWS

CHERRY SWIRL FUDGE

1/2 cup butter
1/4 cup light corn syrup
1/4 teaspoon baking soda
1/2 teaspoon vanilla extract

Place popcorn in a large bowl; set aside. In a saucepan, combine the sugar, butter and corn syrup. Bring to a boil over medium heat; boil and stir until the mixture is golden, about 2 minutes.

Remove from the heat; stir in baking soda and vanilla. Pour over popcorn and toss to coat. Cool slightly; break apart while warm. Store in an airtight container.

Yield: 3 quarts.

Cherry Swirl Fudge

❄ Taste of Home Test Kitchen

For Christmas fudge with a "twist," give this confection a whirl! Our kitchen staff used vanilla chips instead of chocolate and added fruit flavoring.

1-1/2 teaspoons butter
1 package (10 to 12 ounces) vanilla *or* white chips
1 can (16 ounces) *or* 2 cups vanilla frosting
1 teaspoon cherry *or* almond extract
4 drops red liquid food coloring

Line an 8-in. square pan with foil; butter the foil with 1-1/2 teaspoons butter. In a heavy saucepan, melt chips over very low heat, stirring frequently. Or microwave at 70% power for 45 seconds; stir. Microwave in 10- to 20-second intervals or until melted. Remove from the heat; stir in the frosting and extract until blended. Pour into prepared pan.

Randomly place drops of food coloring over fudge; cut through fudge with a knife to swirl. Cover and refrigerate for 4 hours or until firm before cutting into squares.

Yield: 5 dozen.

Editor's Note: This recipe was tested in a 1,100-watt microwave.

Vanilla Popcorn

❄ Carolyn Roney, Scipio Center, New York

If you travel to see friends or family during the holidays, you'll love this tasty treat. It's the perfect snack to nibble on during road trips, and it's easy, too, because it can be ready in about 10 minutes.

3 quarts popped popcorn
1 cup sugar

Peanut Butter Candy

❄ Deloris Morrow, Lake City, Iowa

During the holidays, I make a lot of candy for family and friends, and this simple recipe is a favorite. The white chocolate and chunky peanut butter make a perfect blend.

1/2 teaspoon butter
1-1/4 pounds white candy coating, cut into chunks
1-1/2 cups chunky peanut butter

Line a 9-in. square pan with foil; butter the foil with 1/2 teaspoon butter and set aside. In a microwave-safe bowl, microwave candy coating, uncovered on high for 45 seconds; stir. Microwave 1 to 1-1/2 minutes longer, stirring every 30 seconds, or until candy coating is melted and mixture is smooth. Stir in peanut butter until melted. Transfer to prepared pan. Cool to room temperature. Cut into squares.

Yield: about 1-1/2 pounds.

Editor's Note: This recipe was tested in a 1,100-watt microwave.

PEANUT BUTTER CANDY

CHEWY APPLE CANDIES

Chewy Apple Candies

❄ Roberta Dillinger, Topeka, Kansas

This chewy, fruity candy is a refreshing change of pace from traditional chocolates and fudge. It keeps well in the refrigerator—if you have any left over!

1-1/4 cups raspberry- *or* cinnamon-flavored
      applesauce, *divided*
  2 envelopes unflavored gelatin
  2 cups sugar
  2 teaspoons vanilla extract
  1 cup coarsely chopped walnuts
1/2 cup confectioners' sugar

In a large bowl, combine 1/2 cup applesauce and gelatin; set aside to soften. In a 2-qt. saucepan, bring sugar and remaining applesauce to a boil. Add gelatin mixture; return to boiling. Boil for 15 minutes, stirring constantly. Remove from the heat; stir in vanilla and nuts.

Pour into a buttered 8-in. square pan. Cover and chill overnight. Cut into 1-1/2-in. x 1/2-in. pieces; roll in confectioners' sugar. Refrigerate for several hours. Store in an airtight container in the refrigerator.

Yield: about 7 dozen.

Soft & Chewy Caramels

❄ Darlene Edinger, Turtle Lake, North Dakota

This candy is a must at our house for Christmas. We raised our children on nutritious meals made of simple ingredients. Now I enjoy making special treats like this candy for our eight grandchildren.

  2 cups sugar
  1 cup light corn syrup

  2 cups half-and-half cream, *divided*
  1 cup butter, cubed
  1 teaspoon vanilla extract

Line a 13-in. x 9-in. x 2-in. pan with foil; butter the foil. Set aside. In a Dutch oven, combine the sugar, corn syrup and 1 cup cream. Bring to a boil over medium heat, stirring constantly. Slowly stir in remaining cream. Cook over medium heat until a candy thermometer reads 250° (hard-ball stage), stirring frequently. Remove from the heat; stir in butter and vanilla until well mixed, about 5 minutes.

Pour into prepared pan. Cool. Remove foil from pan; cut candy into 1-in. squares. Wrap individually in waxed paper; twist ends.

Yield: 2 pounds.

Butterscotch Taffy

❄ Teri Lindquist, Wildwood, Illinois

It's a good thing this recipe isn't a lot of fuss—the soft, tempting taffy gets snatched up so fast, I sometimes don't even get to wrap the pieces!

1/2 cup butter
 48 large marshmallows
  1 tablespoon water
1/2 teaspoon salt
  2 cups (12 ounces) butterscotch chips

In a heavy saucepan, combine butter, marshmallows, water and salt; cook and stir over low heat until smooth. Add chips; stir until melted. Pour into a buttered 8-in. square baking pan; cool. Cut into 1-in. squares. Wrap individually in waxed paper; twist ends.

Yield: about 5 dozen.

BUTTERSCOTCH TAFFY

MIXED NUT BRITTLE

Mixed Nut Brittle

❄ Norma Francel, Edwardsburg, Michigan

Nut fanciers have a lot to love about this irresistible brittle. The variety of nuts is what makes it so different. It's one of the first sweet treats to appear on my Christmas candy tray...and also the first to disappear!

1-1/2	teaspoons plus 3 tablespoons butter, *divided*
1-1/2	cups sugar
1	cup water
1	cup light corn syrup
1	can (10 ounces) mixed nuts without peanuts
1	teaspoon vanilla extract
1-1/2	teaspoons baking soda

Butter a baking sheet with 1-1/2 teaspoons of butter; set aside. In a large saucepan, combine the sugar, water and corn syrup. Cook over medium heat until a candy thermometer reads 270° (soft-crack stage), stirring occasionally.

Add nuts; cook and stir until the mixture reaches 300° (hard-crack stage). Remove from the heat; stir in vanilla and remaining butter. Add baking soda and stir vigorously.

Quickly pour onto prepared baking sheet. Spread with a buttered metal spatula to 1/4-in. thickness. Cool before breaking into pieces. Store in an airtight container.

Yield: about 1-3/4 pounds.

Editor's Note: We recommend that you test your candy thermometer before each use by bringing water to a boil; the thermometer should read 212°. Adjust your recipe temperature up or down based on your test.

Pulled Taffy Candy Canes

❄ Sheryl O'Danne, Port Townsend, Washington

My grandmother and great grandmother both made these at Christmastime. The soft and chewy canes have a great minty flavor, and they're especially nice because the whole family can pitch in to prepare them.

2	cups sugar
1/2	cup light corn syrup
1/2	cup water
1/4	teaspoon cream of tartar
3/4	teaspoon peppermint extract
1	teaspoon red food coloring

In a large heavy saucepan over low heat, cook sugar, corn syrup, water and cream of tartar until sugar dissolves, stirring frequently. Increase heat to medium and cook until candy thermometer reads 265° (hard-ball stage), stirring occasionally. Remove from the heat; add extract.

Pour half into a buttered 15-in. x 10-in. x 1-in. pan. Add food coloring to remaining mixture; mix well. Pour into another buttered 15-in. x 10-in. x 1-in. pan. Cool 5 minutes or until cool enough to handle. Butter fingers; quickly pull half of the white or red at a time until firm but pliable (the white portion will have a milky color).

When taffy is ready for cutting, pull into a 1/4-in. rope. Cut into 6-in. pieces. Twist red and white pieces together; form into canes. Place canes on waxed paper-lined baking sheets. Cool.

Yield: 1 to 1-1/2 dozen.

PULLED TAFFY CANDY CANES

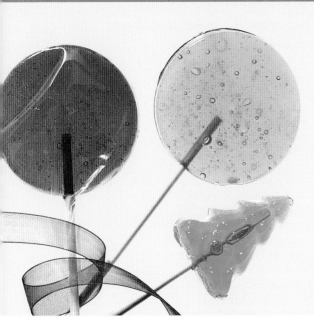

Old-Fashioned Lollipops

❄ **Penny Reifenrath, Wynot, Nebraska**

Kids of all ages will savor these fun, fruity lollipops. The recipe belonged to my late sister-in-law, and every Christmas our family makes them in a rainbow of jewel colors in her memory. They're great stocking stuffers!

1	cup light corn syrup
2/3	cup sugar
1-1/2	teaspoons lemon, apple *or* cherry flavoring
1/8	teaspoon yellow, green *or* red liquid food coloring

In a heavy saucepan, combine corn syrup and sugar. Bring to a boil over medium heat, stirring occasionally. Cover and cook for 3 minutes to dissolve sugar crystals. Uncover and cook over medium-high heat, without stirring, until a candy thermometer reads 300° (hard-crack stage).

Remove from the heat; stir in flavoring and food coloring, keeping face away from mixture as odor is very strong. Immediately pour into prepared molds. Let cool before removing.

Yield: 1 dozen.

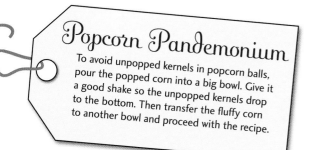

Popcorn Pandemonium

To avoid unpopped kernels in popcorn balls, pour the popped corn into a big bowl. Give it a good shake so the unpopped kernels drop to the bottom. Then transfer the fluffy corn to another bowl and proceed with the recipe.

Candy Cane Popcorn Balls

❄ **Rebecca Gove, Cape Neddick, Maine**

Every Christmas my mother and I made these popcorn balls for family and friends. Now my husband and I happily carry on the tradition.

4	quarts popped popcorn
2	teaspoons water
1	teaspoon baking soda
1/2	teaspoon vanilla extract
1	cup light corn syrup
1/4	cup butter
2	cups sugar
24	miniature candy canes

Place popcorn in a large greased bowl or roasting pan; set aside. In a small bowl, combine the water, baking soda and vanilla; set aside.

In a heavy saucepan, combine corn syrup and butter; heat over medium heat until butter is melted. Add sugar; cook and stir until sugar is dissolved and mixture comes to a boil. Cook and stir until a candy thermometer reaches 230° (thread stage), about 2 minutes.

Remove from heat. Stir in vanilla mixture (mixture will foam) until blended. Immediately pour over popcorn, stirring to coat evenly. Cool for about 5 minutes, stirring several times.

When cool enough to handle, firmly shape with buttered hands into 2-in. balls. Insert straight end of candy cane in the center of each ball.

Yield: 2 dozen.

Editor's Note: We recommend that you test your candy thermometer before each use by bringing water to a boil; the thermometer should read 212°. Adjust your recipe temperature up or down based on your test.

CANDY CANE POPCORN BALLS

General Recipe Index

This index lists every recipe by food category and/or major ingredient, so you can easily locate recipes to suit your needs.

Alphabetical Index

This index lists every recipe in alphabetical order so you can easily find your favorite recipes.